Children Act 2004

CHAPTER 31

Explanatory Notes are available separately

AF719454

GRAN*GIS* UK Publishing

Adapted and published by GRANGIS (Grand Register Library).
Online: www.grangis.com
E-mail: contact@grangis.com

In this version:
ISBN: 979-8-88559-043-3

Note: This is the original version (as it was originally enacted). Title, sub-title and the generated date is as marked on the pages.

Children Act 2004

CHAPTER 31

CONTENTS

PART 1

CHILDREN'S COMMISSIONER

PART 2

CHILDREN'S SERVICES IN ENGLAND

General

Local Safeguarding Children Boards

PART 5

MISCELLANEOUS

PART 6

GENERAL

Children Act 2004

2004 CHAPTER 31

An Act to make provision for the establishment of a Children's Commissioner; to make provision about services provided to and for children and young people by local authorities and other persons; to make provision in relation to Wales about advisory and support services relating to family proceedings; to make provision about private fostering, child minding and day care, adoption review panels, the defence of reasonable punishment, the making of grants as respects children and families, child safety orders, the Children's Commissioner for Wales, the publication of material relating to children involved in certain legal proceedings and the disclosure by the Inland Revenue of information relating to children. [15th November 2004]

BE IT ENACTED by the Queen's most Excellent Majesty, by and with the advice and consent of the Lords Spiritual and Temporal, and Commons, in this present Parliament assembled, and by the authority of the same, as follows:—

PART 1

CHILDREN'S COMMISSIONER

1 Establishment

(1) There is to be an office of Children's Commissioner.

(2) Schedule 1 has effect with respect to the Children's Commissioner.

2 General function

(1) The Children's Commissioner has the function of promoting awareness of the views and interests of children in England.

(2) The Children's Commissioner may in particular under this section—

(a) encourage persons exercising functions or engaged in activities affecting children to take account of their views and interests;
(b) advise the Secretary of State on the views and interests of children;
(c) consider or research the operation of complaints procedures so far as relating to children;
(d) consider or research any other matter relating to the interests of children;
(e) publish a report on any matter considered or researched by him under this section.

(3) The Children's Commissioner is to be concerned in particular under this section with the views and interests of children so far as relating to the following aspects of their well-being—
(a) physical and mental health and emotional well-being;
(b) protection from harm and neglect;
(c) education, training and recreation;
(d) the contribution made by them to society;
(e) social and economic well-being.

(4) The Children's Commissioner must take reasonable steps to involve children in the discharge of his function under this section, and in particular to—
(a) ensure that children are made aware of his function and how they may communicate with him; and
(b) consult children, and organisations working with children, on the matters he proposes to consider or research under subsection (2)(c) or (d).

(5) Where the Children's Commissioner publishes a report under this section he must, if and to the extent that he considers it appropriate, also publish the report in a version which is suitable for children (or, if the report relates to a particular group of children, for those children).

(6) The Children's Commissioner must for the purposes of subsection (4) have particular regard to groups of children who do not have other adequate means by which they can make their views known.

(7) The Children's Commissioner is not under this section to conduct an investigation of the case of an individual child.

(8) The Children's Commissioner or a person authorised by him may for the purposes of his function under this section at any reasonable time—
(a) enter any premises, other than a private dwelling, for the purposes of interviewing any child accommodated or cared for there; and
(b) if the child consents, interview the child in private.

(9) Any person exercising functions under any enactment must supply the Children's Commissioner with such information in that person's possession relating to those functions as the Children's Commissioner may reasonably request for the purposes of his function under this section (provided that the information is information which that person may, apart from this subsection, lawfully disclose to him).

(10) Where the Children's Commissioner has published a report under this section containing recommendations in respect of any person exercising functions under any enactment, he may require that person to state in writing, within such period as the

Children's Commissioner may reasonably require, what action the person has taken or proposes to take in response to the recommendations.

(11) In considering for the purpose of his function under this section what constitutes the interests of children (generally or so far as relating to a particular matter) the Children's Commissioner must have regard to the United Nations Convention on the Rights of the Child.

(12) In subsection (11) the reference to the United Nations Convention on the Rights of the Child is to the Convention on the Rights of the Child adopted by the General Assembly of the United Nations on 20th November 1989, subject to any reservations, objections or interpretative declarations by the United Kingdom for the time being in force.

3 Inquiries initiated by Commissioner

(1) Where the Children's Commissioner considers that the case of an individual child in England raises issues of public policy of relevance to other children, he may hold an inquiry into that case for the purpose of investigating and making recommendations about those issues.

(2) The Children's Commissioner may only conduct an inquiry under this section if he is satisfied that the inquiry would not duplicate work that is the function of another person (having consulted such persons as he considers appropriate).

(3) Before holding an inquiry under this section the Children's Commissioner must consult the Secretary of State.

(4) The Children's Commissioner may, if he thinks fit, hold an inquiry under this section, or any part of it, in private.

(5) As soon as possible after completing an inquiry under this section the Children's Commissioner must—

(a) publish a report containing his recommendations; and

(b) send a copy to the Secretary of State.

(6) The report need not identify any individual child if the Children's Commissioner considers that it would be undesirable for the identity of the child to be made public.

(7) Where the Children's Commissioner has published a report under this section containing recommendations in respect of any person exercising functions under any enactment, he may require that person to state in writing, within such period as the Children's Commissioner may reasonably require, what action the person has taken or proposes to take in response to the recommendations.

(8) Subsections (2) and (3) of section 250 of the Local Government Act 1972 (c. 70) apply for the purposes of an inquiry held under this section with the substitution for references to the person appointed to hold the inquiry of references to the Children's Commissioner.

4 Other inquiries held by Commissioner

(1) Where the Secretary of State considers that the case of an individual child in England raises issues of relevance to other children, he may direct the Children's Commissioner to hold an inquiry into that case.

(2) The Children's Commissioner may, if he thinks fit, hold an inquiry under this section, or any part of it, in private.

(3) The Children's Commissioner must, as soon as possible after the completion of an inquiry under this section, make a report in relation to the inquiry and send a copy to the Secretary of State.

(4) The Secretary of State must, subject to subsection (5), publish each report received by him under this section as soon as possible.

(5) Where a report made under this section identifies an individual child and the Secretary of State considers that it would be undesirable for the identity of the child to be made public—

(a) the Secretary of State may make such amendments to the report as are necessary to protect the identity of the child and publish the amended report only; or

(b) if he considers that it is not possible to publish the report without identifying the child, he need not publish the report.

(6) The Secretary of State must lay a copy of each report published by him under this section before each House of Parliament.

(7) Subsections (2) to (5) of section 250 of the Local Government Act 1972 (c. 70) apply for the purposes of an inquiry held under this section.

5 Functions of Commissioner in Wales

(1) The Children's Commissioner has the function of promoting awareness of the views and interests of children in Wales, except in so far as relating to any matter falling within the remit of the Children's Commissioner for Wales under section 72B, 73 or 74 of the Care Standards Act 2000 (c. 14).

(2) Subsections (2) to (12) of section 2 apply in relation to the function of the Children's Commissioner under subsection (1) above as in relation to his function under that section.

(3) In discharging his function under subsection (1) above the Children's Commissioner must take account of the views of, and any work undertaken by, the Children's Commissioner for Wales.

(4) Where the Children's Commissioner considers that the case of an individual child in Wales raises issues of public policy of relevance to other children, other than issues relating to a matter referred to in subsection (1) above, he may hold an inquiry into that case for the purpose of investigating and making recommendations about those issues.

(5) Subsections (2) to (8) of section 3 apply in relation to an inquiry under subsection (4) above.

(6) Where the Secretary of State considers that the case of an individual child in Wales raises issues of relevance to other children, other than issues relating to a matter referred to in subsection (1) above, he may direct the Children's Commissioner to hold an inquiry into that case.

(7) Subsections (2) to (7) of section 4 apply in relation to an inquiry under subsection (6) above.

6 Functions of Commissioner in Scotland

(1) The Children's Commissioner has the function of promoting awareness of the views and interests of children in Scotland in relation to reserved matters.

(2) Subsections (2) to (12) of section 2 apply in relation to the function of the Children's Commissioner under subsection (1) above as in relation to his function under that section.

(3) In discharging his function under subsection (1) above the Children's Commissioner must take account of the views of, and any work undertaken by, the Commissioner for Children and Young People in Scotland.

(4) Where the Children's Commissioner considers that the case of an individual child in Scotland raises issues of public policy of relevance to other children in relation to a reserved matter, he may hold an inquiry into that case for the purpose of investigating and making recommendations about those issues.

(5) Subsections (2) to (7) of section 3 apply in relation to an inquiry under subsection (4) above.

(6) Subsections (3) to (5) of section 210 of the Local Government (Scotland) Act 1973 (c. 65) apply for the purposes of an inquiry under subsection (4) above with the substitution of references to the Children's Commissioner for references to the person appointed to hold the inquiry.

(7) Where the Secretary of State considers that the case of an individual child in Scotland raises issues of relevance to other children in relation to a reserved matter, he may direct the Children's Commissioner to hold an inquiry into that case.

(8) Subsections (2) to (6) of section 4 apply in relation to an inquiry under subsection (7) above.

(9) Subsections (3) to (8) of section 210 of the Local Government (Scotland) Act 1973 apply for the purposes of an inquiry under subsection (7) above with the substitution (notwithstanding the provisions of section 53 of the Scotland Act 1998 (c. 46) (general transfer of functions to the Scottish Ministers)) of references to the Secretary of State for references to the Minister.

(10) In this section, "reserved matter" has the same meaning as in the Scotland Act 1998 (see section 30 of and Schedule 5 to that Act).

7 Functions of Commissioner in Northern Ireland

(1) The Children's Commissioner has the function of promoting awareness of the views and interests of children in Northern Ireland in relation to excepted matters.

(2) Subsections (2) to (12) of section 2 apply in relation to the function of the Children's Commissioner under subsection (1) above as in relation to his function under that section.

(3) In discharging his function under subsection (1) above the Children's Commissioner must take account of the views of, and any work undertaken by, the Commissioner for Children and Young People for Northern Ireland.

(4) Where the Children's Commissioner considers that the case of an individual child in Northern Ireland raises issues of public policy which are of relevance to other children

in relation to an excepted matter, he may hold an inquiry into that case for the purpose of investigating and making recommendations about those issues.

(5) Subsections (2) to (7) of section 3 apply in relation to an inquiry under subsection (4) above.

(6) Paragraphs 2 to 5 of Schedule 8 to the Health and Personal Social Services (Northern Ireland) Order 1972 (S.I. 1972/1265 (N.I.14)) apply for the purposes of an inquiry under subsection (4) above with the substitution of references to the Children's Commissioner for references to the person appointed to hold the inquiry.

(7) Where the Secretary of State considers that the case of an individual child in Northern Ireland raises issues of relevance to other children in relation to an excepted matter, he may direct the Children's Commissioner to hold an inquiry into that case.

(8) Subsections (2) to (6) of section 4 apply in relation to an inquiry under subsection (7) above.

(9) Paragraphs 2 to 8 of Schedule 8 to the Health and Personal Social Services (Northern Ireland) Order 1972 (S.I. 1972/1265 (N.I.14)) apply for the purposes of an inquiry under subsection (7) above with the substitution of references to the Secretary of State for references to the Ministry.

(10) In this section, "excepted matter" has the same meaning as in the Northern Ireland Act 1998 (c. 47).

8 Annual reports

(1) As soon as possible after the end of each financial year the Children's Commissioner must make a report on—

- (a) the way in which he has discharged his functions under this Part, other than functions of holding inquiries;
- (b) what he has found in the course of exercising those functions during the year; and
- (c) the matters he intends to consider or research in the next financial year.

(2) The Children's Commissioner must in particular under subsection (1)(a) include an account of the steps taken by him to involve in the discharge of the functions referred to in that provision the children in relation to whom those functions are exercised.

(3) Where the Children's Commissioner makes a report under this section—

- (a) he must send a copy to the Secretary of State; and
- (b) the Secretary of State must as soon as possible lay a copy before each House of Parliament.

(4) The Children's Commissioner must publish a report under this section as soon as possible after the Secretary of State has laid it before each House of Parliament.

(5) The Children's Commissioner must also, to the extent that he considers appropriate, publish any report made under this section in a version which is suitable for children.

(6) In this section, "financial year" has the same meaning as in paragraph 8 of Schedule 1.

9 Care leavers and young persons with learning disabilities

(1) This section applies for the purposes of this Part, other than section 2(11) and (12).

(2) Any reference to a child includes, in addition to a person under the age of 18, a person aged 18, 19 or 20 who—

(a) has been looked after by a local authority at any time after attaining the age of 16; or

(b) has a learning disability.

(3) For the purposes of subsection (2)—

a person is "looked after by a local authority" if—

(a) for the purposes of the Children Act 1989 (c. 41), he is looked after by a local authority in England and Wales;

(b) for the purposes of the Children (Scotland) Act 1995 (c. 36), he is looked after by a local authority in Scotland;

(c) for the purposes of the Children (Northern Ireland) Order 1995 (S.I.1995/755 (N.I.2)), he is looked after by an authority in Northern Ireland;

"learning disability" means a state of arrested or incomplete development of mind which induces significant impairment of intelligence and social functioning.

PART 2

CHILDREN'S SERVICES IN ENGLAND

General

10 Co-operation to improve well-being

(1) Each children's services authority in England must make arrangements to promote co-operation between—

(a) the authority;

(b) each of the authority's relevant partners; and

(c) such other persons or bodies as the authority consider appropriate, being persons or bodies of any nature who exercise functions or are engaged in activities in relation to children in the authority's area.

(2) The arrangements are to be made with a view to improving the well-being of children in the authority's area so far as relating to—

(a) physical and mental health and emotional well-being;

(b) protection from harm and neglect;

(c) education, training and recreation;

(d) the contribution made by them to society;

(e) social and economic well-being.

(3) In making arrangements under this section a children's services authority in England must have regard to the importance of parents and other persons caring for children in improving the well-being of children.

(4) For the purposes of this section each of the following is a relevant partner of a children's services authority in England—

(a) where the authority is a county council for an area for which there is also a district council, the district council;

(b) the police authority and the chief officer of police for a police area any part of which falls within the area of the children's services authority;

(c) a local probation board for an area any part of which falls within the area of the authority;

(d) a youth offending team for an area any part of which falls within the area of the authority;

(e) a Strategic Health Authority and Primary Care Trust for an area any part of which falls within the area of the authority;

(f) a person providing services under section 114 of the Learning and Skills Act 2000 (c. 21) in any part of the area of the authority;

(g) the Learning and Skills Council for England.

(5) The relevant partners of a children's services authority in England must co-operate with the authority in the making of arrangements under this section.

(6) A children's services authority in England and any of their relevant partners may for the purposes of arrangements under this section—

(a) provide staff, goods, services, accommodation or other resources;

(b) establish and maintain a pooled fund.

(7) For the purposes of subsection (6) a pooled fund is a fund—

(a) which is made up of contributions by the authority and the relevant partner or partners concerned; and

(b) out of which payments may be made towards expenditure incurred in the discharge of functions of the authority and functions of the relevant partner or partners.

(8) A children's services authority in England and each of their relevant partners must in exercising their functions under this section have regard to any guidance given to them for the purpose by the Secretary of State.

(9) Arrangements under this section may include arrangements relating to—

(a) persons aged 18 and 19;

(b) persons over the age of 19 who are receiving services under sections 23C to 24D of the Children Act 1989 (c. 41);

(c) persons over the age of 19 but under the age of 25 who have a learning difficulty, within the meaning of section 13 of the Learning and Skills Act 2000, and are receiving services under that Act.

11 Arrangements to safeguard and promote welfare

(1) This section applies to each of the following—

(a) a children's services authority in England;

(b) a district council which is not such an authority;

(c) a Strategic Health Authority;

(d) a Special Health Authority, so far as exercising functions in relation to England, designated by order made by the Secretary of State for the purposes of this section;
(e) a Primary Care Trust;
(f) an NHS trust all or most of whose hospitals, establishments and facilities are situated in England;
(g) an NHS foundation trust;
(h) the police authority and chief officer of police for a police area in England;
(i) the British Transport Police Authority, so far as exercising functions in relation to England;
(j) a local probation board for an area in England;
(k) a youth offending team for an area in England;
(l) the governor of a prison or secure training centre in England (or, in the case of a contracted out prison or secure training centre, its director);
(m) any person to the extent that he is providing services under section 114 of the Learning and Skills Act 2000 (c. 21).

(2) Each person and body to whom this section applies must make arrangements for ensuring that—
(a) their functions are discharged having regard to the need to safeguard and promote the welfare of children; and
(b) any services provided by another person pursuant to arrangements made by the person or body in the discharge of their functions are provided having regard to that need.

(3) In the case of a children's services authority in England, the reference in subsection (2) to functions of the authority does not include functions to which section 175 of the Education Act 2002 (c. 32) applies.

(4) Each person and body to whom this section applies must in discharging their duty under this section have regard to any guidance given to them for the purpose by the Secretary of State.

12 Information databases

(1) The Secretary of State may for the purpose of arrangements under section 10 or 11 above or under section 175 of the Education Act 2002—
(a) by regulations require children's services authorities in England to establish and operate databases containing information in respect of persons to whom such arrangements relate;
(b) himself establish and operate, or make arrangements for the operation and establishment of, one or more databases containing such information.

(2) The Secretary of State may for the purposes of arrangements under subsection (1)(b) by regulations establish a body corporate to establish and operate one or more databases.

(3) A database under this section may only include information falling within subsection (4) in relation to a person to whom arrangements specified in subsection (1) relate.

(4) The information referred to in subsection (3) is information of the following descriptions in relation to a person—

(a) his name, address, gender and date of birth;

(b) a number identifying him;

(c) the name and contact details of any person with parental responsibility for him (within the meaning of section 3 of the Children Act 1989 (c. 41)) or who has care of him at any time;

(d) details of any education being received by him (including the name and contact details of any educational institution attended by him);

(e) the name and contact details of any person providing primary medical services in relation to him under Part 1 of the National Health Service Act 1977 (c. 49);

(f) the name and contact details of any person providing to him services of such description as the Secretary of State may by regulations specify;

(g) information as to the existence of any cause for concern in relation to him;

(h) information of such other description, not including medical records or other personal records, as the Secretary of State may by regulations specify.

(5) The Secretary of State may by regulations make provision in relation to the establishment and operation of any database or databases under this section.

(6) Regulations under subsection (5) may in particular make provision—

(a) as to the information which must or may be contained in any database under this section (subject to subsection (3));

(b) requiring a person or body specified in subsection (7) to disclose information for inclusion in the database;

(c) permitting a person or body specified in subsection (8) to disclose information for inclusion in the database;

(d) permitting or requiring the disclosure of information included in any such database;

(e) permitting or requiring any person to be given access to any such database for the purpose of adding or reading information;

(f) as to the conditions on which such access must or may be given;

(g) as to the length of time for which information must or may be retained;

(h) as to procedures for ensuring the accuracy of information included in any such database;

(i) in a case where a database is established by virtue of subsection (1)(b), requiring children's services authorities in England to participate in the operation of the database.

(7) The persons and bodies referred to in subsection (6)(b) are—

(a) the persons and bodies specified in section 11(1);

(b) the Learning and Skills Council for England;

(c) the governing body of a maintained school in England (within the meaning of section 175 of the Education Act 2002 (c. 32));

(d) the governing body of an institution in England within the further education sector (within the meaning of that section);

(e) the proprietor of an independent school in England (within the meaning of the Education Act 1996 (c. 56));

(f) a person or body of such other description as the Secretary of State may by regulations specify.

(8) The persons and bodies referred to in subsection (6)(c) are—

(a) a person registered in England for child minding or the provision of day care under Part 10A of the Children Act 1989 (c. 41);

(b) a voluntary organisation exercising functions or engaged in activities in relation to persons to whom arrangements specified in subsection (1) relate;

(c) the Commissioners of Inland Revenue;

(d) a registered social landlord;

(e) a person or body of such other description as the Secretary of State may by regulations specify.

(9) The Secretary of State may provide information for inclusion in a database under this section.

(10) The provision which may be made under subsection (6)(e) includes provision for a person of a description specified in the regulations to determine what must or may be done under the regulations.

(11) Regulations under subsection (5) may also provide that anything which may be done under regulations under subsection (6)(c) to (e) or (9) may be done notwithstanding any rule of common law which prohibits or restricts the disclosure of information.

(12) Any person or body establishing or operating a database under this section must in the establishment or operation of the database have regard to any guidance, and comply with any direction, given to that person or body by the Secretary of State.

(13) Guidance or directions under subsection (12) may in particular relate to—

(a) the management of a database under this section;

(b) the technical specifications for any such database;

(c) the security of any such database;

(d) the transfer and comparison of information between databases under this section;

(e) the giving of advice in relation to rights under the Data Protection Act 1998 (c. 29).

Local Safeguarding Children Boards

13 Establishment of LSCBs

(1) Each children's services authority in England must establish a Local Safeguarding Children Board for their area.

(2) A Board established under this section must include such representative or representatives of—

(a) the authority by which it is established, and

(b) each Board partner of that authority,

as the Secretary of State may by regulations prescribe.

(3) For the purposes of this section each of the following is a Board partner of a children's services authority in England—

(a) where the authority is a county council for an area for which there is also a district council, the district council;

(b) the chief officer of police for a police area any part of which falls within the area of the authority;

(c) a local probation board for an area any part of which falls within the area of the authority;

(d) a youth offending team for an area any part of which falls within the area of the authority;

(e) a Strategic Health Authority and a Primary Care Trust for an area any part of which falls within the area of the authority;

(f) an NHS trust and an NHS foundation trust all or most of whose hospitals, establishments and facilities are situated in the area of the authority;

(g) a person providing services under section 114 of the Learning and Skills Act 2000 (c. 21) in any part of the area of the authority;

(h) the Children and Family Court Advisory and Support Service;

(i) the governor of any secure training centre in the area of the authority (or, in the case of a contracted out secure training centre, its director);

(j) the governor of any prison in the area of the authority which ordinarily detains children (or, in the case of a contracted out prison, its director).

(4) A children's services authority in England must take reasonable steps to ensure that the Local Safeguarding Children Board established by them includes representatives of relevant persons and bodies of such descriptions as may be prescribed by the Secretary of State in regulations.

(5) A Local Safeguarding Children Board established under this section may also include representatives of such other relevant persons or bodies as the authority by which it is established consider, after consulting their Board partners, should be represented on it.

(6) For the purposes of subsections (4) and (5), relevant persons and bodies are persons and bodies of any nature exercising functions or engaged in activities relating to children in the area of the authority in question.

(7) In the establishment and operation of a Local Safeguarding Children Board under this section—

(a) the authority establishing it must co-operate with each of their Board partners; and

(b) each Board partner must co-operate with the authority.

(8) Two or more children's services authorities in England may discharge their respective duties under subsection (1) by establishing a Local Safeguarding Children Board for their combined area (and where they do so, any reference in this section or sections 14 to 16 to the authority establishing the Board shall be read as a reference to the authorities establishing it).

14 Functions and procedure of LSCBs

(1) The objective of a Local Safeguarding Children Board established under section 13 is—

(a) to co-ordinate what is done by each person or body represented on the Board for the purposes of safeguarding and promoting the welfare of children in the area of the authority by which it is established; and

(b) to ensure the effectiveness of what is done by each such person or body for those purposes.

(2) A Local Safeguarding Children Board established under section 13 is to have such functions in relation to its objective as the Secretary of State may by regulations prescribe (which may in particular include functions of review or investigation).

(3) The Secretary of State may by regulations make provision as to the procedures to be followed by a Local Safeguarding Children Board established under section 13.

15 Funding of LSCBs

(1) Any person or body specified in subsection (3) may make payments towards expenditure incurred by, or for purposes connected with, a Local Safeguarding Children Board established under section 13—

(a) by making the payments directly; or

(b) by contributing to a fund out of which the payments may be made.

(2) Any person or body specified in subsection (3) may provide staff, goods, services, accommodation or other resources for purposes connected with a Local Safeguarding Children Board established under section 13.

(3) The persons and bodies referred to in subsections (1) and (2) are—

(a) the children's services authority in England by which the Board is established;

(b) any person who is a Board partner of the authority under section 13(3)(a) to (h);

(c) in a case where the governor of a secure training centre or prison is a Board partner of the authority, the Secretary of State; and

(d) in a case where the director of a contracted out secure training centre or prison is a Board partner of the authority, the contractor.

16 LSCBs: supplementary

(1) The Secretary of State may by regulations make provision as to the functions of children's services authorities in England relating to Local Safeguarding Children Boards established by them.

(2) A children's services authority in England and each of their Board partners must, in exercising their functions relating to a Local Safeguarding Children Board, have regard to any guidance given to them for the purpose by the Secretary of State.

Local authority administration

17 Children and young people's plans

(1) The Secretary of State may by regulations require a children's services authority in England from time to time to prepare and publish a plan setting out the authority's strategy for discharging their functions in relation to children and relevant young persons.

(2) Regulations under this section may in particular make provision as to—

(a) the matters to be dealt with in a plan under this section;

(b) the period to which a plan under this section is to relate;
(c) when and how a plan under this section must be published;
(d) keeping a plan under this section under review;
(e) consultation to be carried out during preparation of a plan under this section.

(3) The matters for which provision may be made under subsection (2)(a) include in particular—
(a) the arrangements made or to be made under section 10 by a children's services authority in England;
(b) the strategy or proposals in relation to children and relevant young persons of any person or body with whom a children's services authority in England makes or proposes to make such arrangements.

(4) The power to make regulations conferred by this section shall, for the purposes of subsection (1) of section 100 of the Local Government Act 2003 (c. 26), be regarded as included among the powers mentioned in subsection (2) of that section.

(5) In this section "relevant young persons" means persons, other than children, in relation to whom arrangements under section 10 may be made.

18 Director of children's services

(1) A children's services authority in England may, and with effect from the appointed day must, appoint an officer for the purposes of—
(a) the functions conferred on or exercisable by the authority which are specified in subsection (2); and
(b) such other functions conferred on or exercisable by the authority as may be prescribed by the Secretary of State by regulations.

(2) The functions referred to in subsection (1)(a) are—
(a) functions conferred on or exercisable by the authority in their capacity as a local education authority;
(b) functions conferred on or exercisable by the authority which are social services functions (within the meaning of the Local Authority Social Services Act 1970 (c. 42)), so far as those functions relate to children;
(c) the functions conferred on the authority under sections 23C to 24D of the Children Act 1989 (c. 41) (so far as not falling within paragraph (b));
(d) the functions conferred on the authority under sections 10 to 12 and 17 of this Act; and
(e) any functions exercisable by the authority under section 31 of the Health Act 1999 (c. 8) on behalf of an NHS body (within the meaning of that section), so far as those functions relate to children.

(3) Subsection (2)(a) does not include—
(a) functions under section 120(3) of the Education Reform Act 1988 (c. 40) (functions of LEAs with respect to higher and further education);
(b) functions under section 85(2) and (3) of the Further and Higher Education Act 1992 (c. 13) (finance and government of locally funded further and higher education);
(c) functions under section 15B of the Education Act 1996 (c. 56) or section 23 of the Learning and Skills Act 2000 (c. 21) (education for persons who have attained the age of 19);

(d) functions under section 22 of the Teaching and Higher Education Act 1998 (c. 30) (financial support to students);

(e) such other functions conferred on or exercisable by a children's services authority in England in their capacity as a local education authority as the Secretary of State may by regulations prescribe.

(4) An officer appointed by a children's services authority in England under this section is to be known as their "director of children's services".

(5) The director of children's services appointed by a children's services authority in England may also have responsibilities relating to such functions conferred on or exercisable by the authority, in addition to those specified in subsection (1), as the authority consider appropriate.

(6) The functions in relation to which a director of children's services may have responsibilities by virtue of subsection (5) include those referred to in subsection (3)(a) to (e).

(7) A children's services authority in England must have regard to any guidance given to them by the Secretary of State for the purposes of this section.

(8) Two or more children's services authorities in England may for the purposes of this section, if they consider that the same person can efficiently discharge, for both or all of them, the responsibilities of director of children's services, concur in the appointment of a person as director of children's services for both or all of them.

(9) The amendments in Schedule 2—

(a) have effect, in relation to any authority which appoint a director of children's services before the appointed day, from the day of his appointment; and

(b) on and after the appointed day have effect for all purposes.

(10) In this section, "the appointed day" means such day as the Secretary of State may by order appoint.

19 Lead member for children's services

(1) A children's services authority in England must, in making arrangements for the discharge of—

(a) the functions conferred on or exercisable by the authority specified in section 18(1)(a) and (b), and

(b) such other functions conferred on or exercisable by the authority as the authority consider appropriate,

designate one of their members as their "lead member for children's services".

(2) A children's services authority in England must have regard to any guidance given to them by the Secretary of State for the purposes of subsection (1).

Inspections of children's services

20 Joint area reviews

(1) Any two or more of the persons and bodies to which this section applies must, at the request of the Secretary of State—

(a) conduct, in accordance with a timetable drawn up by them and approved by the Secretary of State, a review of children's services provided in—
   (i) the area of every children's services authority in England;
   (ii) the areas of such children's services authorities in England as may be specified in the request;

(b) conduct a review of such children's services provided in the area of such children's services authority in England as may be specified in the request.

(2) Any two or more of the persons and bodies to which this section applies may conduct a review of any children's services provided in the area of a particular children's services authority in England.

(3) The purpose of a review under this section is to evaluate the extent to which, taken together, the children's services being reviewed improve the well-being of children and relevant young persons (and in particular to evaluate how those services work together to improve their well-being).

(4) The persons and bodies to which this section applies are—
(a) the Chief Inspector of Schools;
(b) the Adult Learning Inspectorate;
(c) the Commission for Social Care Inspection;
(d) the Commission for Healthcare Audit and Inspection;
(e) the Audit Commission for Local Authorities and the National Health Service in England and Wales;
(f) the chief inspector of constabulary;
(g) Her Majesty's Chief Inspector of the National Probation Service for England and Wales;
(h) Her Majesty's Chief Inspector of Court Administration; and
(i) the Chief Inspector of Prisons.

(5) Reviews under this section are to be conducted in accordance with arrangements made by the Chief Inspector of Schools.

(6) Before making arrangements for the purposes of reviews under this section the Chief Inspector of Schools must consult such of the other persons and bodies to which this section applies as he considers appropriate.

(7) The annual report of the Chief Inspector of Schools required by subsection (7)(a) of section 2 of the School Inspections Act 1996 (c. 57) to be made to the Secretary of State must include an account of reviews under this section; and the power conferred by subsection (7)(b) of that section to make other reports to the Secretary of State includes a power to make reports about such reviews.

(8) The Secretary of State may by regulations make provision for the purposes of reviews under this section and in particular provision—
(a) requiring or facilitating the sharing or production of information for the purposes of a review under this section (including provision for the creation of criminal offences);
(b) authorising any person or body conducting a review under this section to enter any premises for the purposes of the review (including provision for the creation of criminal offences);

(c) imposing requirements as to the making of a report on each review under this section;

(d) for the making by such persons as may be specified in or under the regulations of written statements of proposed action in the light of the report and the period within which any such action must or may be taken;

(e) for the provision to members of the public of copies of reports and statements made under paragraphs (c) and (d), and for charging in respect of any such provision;

(f) for the disapplication, in consequence of a requirement under this section, of any requirement under any other enactment to conduct an assessment or to do anything in connection with an assessment.

(9) Regulations under subsection (8) may in particular make provision by applying enactments falling within subsection (10), with or without modification, for the purposes of reviews under this section.

(10) The enactments falling within this subsection are enactments relating to the powers of persons and bodies to which this section applies for the purposes of assessments other than reviews under this section.

(11) Regulations under subsection (8) may make provision authorising or requiring the doing of anything by reference to the determination of a person of a description specified in the regulations.

21 Framework

(1) The Chief Inspector of Schools must devise a Framework for Inspection of Children's Services ("the Framework").

(2) The Framework must, for the purpose specified in subsection (3), set out principles to be applied by any person or body conducting a relevant assessment.

(3) The purpose referred to in subsection (2) is to ensure that relevant assessments properly evaluate and report on the extent to which children's services improve the well-being of children and relevant young persons.

(4) The principles in the Framework may—

(a) include principles relating to the organisation of the results of any relevant assessment;

(b) make different provision for different cases.

(5) For the purposes of subsections (2) to (4) a relevant assessment is an assessment conducted under any enactment in relation to any children's services.

(6) When devising the Framework, the Chief Inspector of Schools must consult the other persons and bodies to which section 20 applies.

(7) The Chief Inspector of Schools must publish the Framework, but before doing so must—

(a) consult such persons and bodies, other than those referred to in subsection (6), as he thinks fit; and

(b) obtain the consent of the Secretary of State.

(8) The Chief Inspector of Schools may at any time revise the Framework (and subsections (6) and (7) apply in relation to revisions to the Framework as to the original Framework).

22 Co-operation and delegation

(1) Each person or body with functions under any enactment of conducting assessments of children's services must for the purposes of those assessments co-operate with other persons or bodies with such functions.

(2) A person or body with functions under any enactment of conducting assessments of children's services may delegate any of those functions to any other person or body with such functions.

23 Sections 20 to 22: interpretation

(1) This section applies for the purposes of sections 20 to 22.

(2) "Assessment" includes an inspection, review, investigation or study.

(3) "Children's services" means—

(a) anything done for or in relation to children and relevant young persons (alone or with other persons)—

(i) in respect of which, apart from section 20, a person or body to which that section applies conducts any kind of assessment, or secures that any kind of assessment is conducted; and

(ii) which is specified in, or is of a description prescribed by, regulations made by the Secretary of State;

(b) any function under sections 10 and 13 to 19; and

(c) any function conferred on a children's services authority under section 12.

(4) "Relevant young persons" means persons, other than children, in relation to whom arrangements under section 10 may be made.

(5) "The Chief Inspector of Schools" means Her Majesty's Chief Inspector of Schools in England.

24 Performance rating of social services

(1) In section 79(2) of the Health and Social Care (Community Health and Standards) Act 2003 (c. 43) (duty of Commission for Social Care Inspection to award a performance rating to a local authority), for the words from "a performance rating" to the end substitute—

"(a) a performance rating to that authority in respect of all the English local authority social services provided by, or pursuant to arrangements made by, that authority—

(i) to or so far as relating to persons under the age of eighteen; or

(ii) under sections 23C to 24D of the Children Act 1989; and

(b) a performance rating to that authority in respect of all other English local authority social services provided by, or pursuant to arrangements made by, that authority."

(2) In section 81(2) of that Act (duty of the Commission to inform the Secretary of State where it awards the lowest performance rating under section 79), for "section 79" substitute "section 79(2)(a) or (b)".

PART 3

CHILDREN'S SERVICES IN WALES

General

25 Co-operation to improve well-being: Wales

(1) Each children's services authority in Wales must make arrangements to promote co-operation between—

(a) the authority;

(b) each of the authority's relevant partners; and

(c) such other persons or bodies as the authority consider appropriate, being persons or bodies of any nature who exercise functions or are engaged in activities in relation to children in the authority's area.

(2) The arrangements are to be made with a view to improving the well-being of children in the authority's area so far as relating to—

(a) physical and mental health and emotional well-being;

(b) protection from harm and neglect;

(c) education, training and recreation;

(d) the contribution made by them to society;

(e) social and economic well-being.

(3) In making arrangements under this section a children's services authority in Wales must have regard to the importance of parents and other persons caring for children in improving the well-being of children.

(4) For the purposes of this section each of the following is the relevant partner of a children's services authority in Wales—

(a) the police authority and the chief officer of police for a police area any part of which falls within the area of the children's services authority;

(b) a local probation board for an area any part of which falls within the area of the authority;

(c) a youth offending team for an area any part of which falls within the area of the authority;

(d) a Local Health Board for an area any part of which falls within the area of the authority;

(e) an NHS trust providing services in the area of the authority;

(f) the National Council for Education and Training for Wales.

(5) The relevant partners of a children's services authority in Wales must co-operate with the authority in the making of arrangements under this section.

(6) A children's services authority in Wales and any of their relevant partners may for the purposes of arrangements under this section—

(a) provide staff, goods, services, accommodation or other resources;
(b) establish and maintain a pooled fund.

(7) For the purposes of subsection (6) a pooled fund is a fund—
(a) which is made up of contributions by the authority and the relevant partner or partners concerned; and
(b) out of which payments may be made towards expenditure incurred in the discharge of functions of the authority and functions of the relevant partner or partners.

(8) A children's services authority in Wales and each of their relevant partners must in exercising their functions under this section have regard to any guidance given to them for the purpose by the Assembly.

(9) The Assembly must obtain the consent of the Secretary of State before giving guidance under subsection (8) at any time after the coming into force of any of paragraphs (a) to (c) of subsection (4).

(10) Arrangements under this section may include arrangements relating to—
(a) persons aged 18 and 19;
(b) persons over the age of 19 who are receiving—
(i) services under sections 23C to 24D of the Children Act 1989 (c. 41); or
(ii) youth support services (within the meaning of section 123 of the Learning and Skills Act 2000 (c. 21)).

26 Children and young people's plans: Wales

(1) The Assembly may by regulations require a children's services authority in Wales from time to time to prepare and publish a plan setting out the authority's strategy for discharging their functions in relation to children and relevant young persons.

(2) Regulations under this section may in particular make provision as to—
(a) the matters to be dealt with in a plan under this section;
(b) the period to which a plan under this section is to relate;
(c) when and how a plan under this section must be published;
(d) keeping a plan under this section under review;
(e) consultation to be carried out before a plan under this section is published;
(f) implementation of a plan under this section.

(3) The matters for which provision may be made under subsection (2)(a) include in particular—
(a) the arrangements made or to be made under section 25 by a children's services authority in Wales;
(b) the strategy or proposals in relation to children and relevant young persons of any person or body with whom a children's services authority in Wales makes or proposes to make such arrangements.

(4) Regulations under this section may require a children's services authority in Wales to obtain the Assembly's approval before publishing a plan under this section; and may provide that the Assembly may modify a plan before approving it.

(5) A children's services authority in Wales must have regard to any guidance given to them by the Assembly in relation to how they are to discharge their functions under regulations under this section.

(6) In this section "relevant young persons" means the persons, in addition to children, in relation to whom arrangements under section 25 may be made.

27 Responsibility for functions under sections 25 and 26

(1) A children's services authority in Wales must—

(a) appoint an officer, to be known as the "lead director for children and young people's services", for the purposes of co-ordinating and overseeing arrangements made under sections 25 and 26; and

(b) designate one of their members, to be known as the "lead member for children and young people's services", to have as his special care the discharge of the authority's functions under those sections.

(2) A Local Health Board must—

(a) appoint an officer, to be known as the Board's "lead officer for children and young people's services", for the purposes of the Board's functions under section 25; and

(b) designate one of the Board's members who is not an officer as its "lead member for children and young people's services" to have the discharge of those functions as his special care.

(3) An NHS trust to which section 25 applies must—

(a) appoint an executive director, to be known as the trust's "lead executive director for children and young people's services", for the purposes of the trust's functions under that section; and

(b) designate one of the trust's non-executive directors as its "lead non-executive director for children and young people's services" to have the discharge of those functions as his special care.

(4) Each children's services authority in Wales, Local Health Board and NHS trust to which section 25 applies must have regard to any guidance given to them by the Assembly in relation to—

(a) their functions under this section;

(b) the responsibilities of the persons appointed or designated by them under this section.

28 Arrangements to safeguard and promote welfare: Wales

(1) This section applies to each of the following—

(a) a children's services authority in Wales;

(b) a Local Health Board;

(c) an NHS trust all or most of whose hospitals, establishments and facilities are situated in Wales;

(d) the police authority and chief officer of police for a police area in Wales;

(e) the British Transport Police Authority, so far as exercising functions in relation to Wales;

(f) a local probation board for an area in Wales;

(g) a youth offending team for an area in Wales;

(h) the governor of a prison or secure training centre in Wales (or, in the case of a contracted out prison or secure training centre, its director);

(i) any person to the extent that he is providing services pursuant to arrangements made by a children's services authority in Wales under section 123(1)(b) of the Learning and Skills Act 2000 (c. 21) (youth support services).

(2) Each person and body to whom this section applies must make arrangements for ensuring that—

(a) their functions are discharged having regard to the need to safeguard and promote the welfare of children; and

(b) any services provided by another person pursuant to arrangements made by the person or body in the discharge of their functions are provided having regard to that need.

(3) In the case of a children's services authority in Wales, the reference in subsection (2) to functions of the authority does not include functions to which section 175 of the Education Act 2002 (c. 32) applies.

(4) The persons and bodies referred to in subsection (1)(a) to (c) and (i) must in discharging their duty under this section have regard to any guidance given to them for the purpose by the Assembly.

(5) The persons and bodies referred to in subsection (1)(d) to (h) must in discharging their duty under this section have regard to any guidance given to them for the purpose by the Secretary of State after consultation with the Assembly.

29 Information databases: Wales

(1) The Assembly may for the purpose of arrangements under section 25 or 28 above or under section 175 of the Education Act 2002—

(a) by regulations require children's services authorities in Wales to establish and operate databases containing information in respect of persons to whom such arrangements relate;

(b) itself establish and operate, or make arrangements for the operation and establishment of, one or more databases containing such information.

(2) The Assembly may for the purposes of arrangements under subsection (1)(b) by regulations establish a body corporate to establish and operate one or more databases.

(3) A database under this section may only include information falling within subsection (4) in relation to a person to whom arrangements specified in subsection (1) relate.

(4) The information referred to in subsection (3) is information of the following descriptions in relation to a person—

(a) his name, address, gender and date of birth;

(b) a number identifying him;

(c) the name and contact details of any person with parental responsibility for him (within the meaning of section 3 of the Children Act 1989 (c. 41)) or who has care of him at any time;

(d) details of any education being received by him (including the name and contact details of any educational institution attended by him);

(e) the name and contact details of any person providing primary medical services in relation to him under Part 1 of the National Health Service Act 1977 (c. 49);

(f) the name and contact details of any person providing to him services of such description as the Assembly may by regulations specify;

(g) information as to the existence of any cause for concern in relation to him;

(h) information of such other description, not including medical records or other personal records, as the Assembly may by regulations specify.

(5) The Assembly may by regulations make provision in relation to the establishment and operation of any database or databases under this section.

(6) Regulations under subsection (5) may in particular make provision—

(a) as to the information which must or may be contained in any database under this section (subject to subsection (3));

(b) requiring a person or body specified in subsection (7) to disclose information for inclusion in the database;

(c) permitting a person or body specified in subsection (8) to disclose information for inclusion in the database;

(d) permitting or requiring the disclosure of information included in any such database;

(e) permitting or requiring any person to be given access to any such database for the purpose of adding or reading information;

(f) as to the conditions on which such access must or may be given;

(g) as to the length of time for which information must or may be retained;

(h) as to procedures for ensuring the accuracy of information included in any such database;

(i) in a case where a database is established by virtue of subsection (1)(b), requiring children's services authorities in Wales to participate in the operation of the database.

(7) The persons and bodies referred to in subsection (6)(b) are—

(a) the persons and bodies specified in section 28(1);

(b) the National Council for Education and Training for Wales;

(c) the governing body of a maintained school in Wales (within the meaning of section 175 of the Education Act 2002 (c. 32));

(d) the governing body of an institution in Wales within the further education sector (within the meaning of that section);

(e) the proprietor of an independent school in Wales (within the meaning of the Education Act 1996 (c. 56));

(f) a person or body of such other description as the Assembly may by regulations specify.

(8) The persons and bodies referred to in subsection (6)(c) are—

(a) a person registered in Wales for child minding or the provision of day care under Part 10A of the Children Act 1989 (c. 41);

(b) a voluntary organisation exercising functions or engaged in activities in relation to persons to whom arrangements specified in subsection (1) relate;

(c) the Commissioners of Inland Revenue;

(d) a registered social landlord;

(e) a person or body of such other description as the Assembly may by regulations specify.

(9) The Assembly and the Secretary of State may provide information for inclusion in a database under this section.

(10) The provision which may be made under subsection (6)(e) includes provision for a person of a description specified in the regulations to determine what must or may be done under the regulations.

(11) Regulations under subsection (5) may also provide that anything which may be done under regulations under subsection (6)(c) to (e) or (9) may be done notwithstanding any rule of common law which prohibits or restricts the disclosure of information.

(12) Regulations under subsections (1)(a) and (5) may only be made with the consent of the Secretary of State.

(13) Any person or body establishing or operating a database under this section must in the establishment or operation of the database have regard to any guidance, and comply with any direction, given to that person by the Assembly.

(14) Guidance or directions under subsection (13) may in particular relate to—

(a) the management of a database under this section;

(b) the technical specifications for any such database;

(c) the security of any such database;

(d) the transfer and comparison of information between databases under this section;

(e) the giving of advice in relation to rights under the Data Protection Act 1998 (c. 29).

30 Inspection of functions under this Part

(1) Chapter 6 of Part 2 of the Health and Social Care (Community Health and Standards) Act 2003 (c. 43) (functions of the Assembly in relation to social services) shall apply as if anything done by a children's services authority in Wales in the exercise of functions to which this section applies were a Welsh local authority social service within the meaning of that Part.

(2) This section applies to the following functions of a children's services authority—

(a) the authority's functions under section 25 or 26, except so far as relating to education, training or youth support services (within the meaning of section 123 of the Learning and Skills Act 2000 (c. 21));

(b) the authority's functions under section 28;

(c) any function conferred on the authority under section 29.

Local Safeguarding Children Boards

31 Establishment of LSCBs in Wales

(1) Each children's services authority in Wales must establish a Local Safeguarding Children Board for their area.

(2) A Board established under this section must include such representative or representatives of—

(a) the authority by which it is established, and

(b) each Board partner of that authority,

as the Assembly may by regulations prescribe.

(3) For the purposes of this section each of the following is a Board partner of a children's services authority in Wales—

(a) the chief officer of police for a police area any part of which falls within the area of the authority;

(b) a local probation board for an area any part of which falls within the area of the authority;

(c) a youth offending team for an area any part of which falls within the area of the authority;

(d) a Local Health Board for an area any part of which falls within the area of the authority;

(e) an NHS trust providing services in the area of the authority;

(f) the governor of any secure training centre within the area of the authority (or, in the case of a contracted out secure training centre, its director);

(g) the governor of any prison in the area of the authority which ordinarily detains children (or, in the case of a contracted out prison, its director).

(4) Regulations under subsection (2) that make provision in relation to a Board partner referred to in subsection (3)(a) to (c), (f) or (g) may only be made with the consent of the Secretary of State.

(5) A children's services authority in Wales must take reasonable steps to ensure that the Local Safeguarding Children Board established by them includes representatives of relevant persons and bodies of such descriptions as may be prescribed by the Assembly in regulations.

(6) A Local Safeguarding Children Board established under this section may also include representatives of such other relevant persons or bodies as the authority by which it is established consider, after consulting their Board partners, should be represented on it.

(7) For the purposes of subsections (5) and (6), relevant persons and bodies are persons and bodies of any nature exercising functions or engaged in activities relating to children in the area of the authority in question.

(8) In the establishment and operation of a Local Safeguarding Children Board under this section—

(a) the authority establishing it must co-operate with each of their Board partners; and

(b) each Board partner must co-operate with the authority.

(9) Two or more children's services authorities in Wales may discharge their respective duties under subsection (1) by establishing a Local Safeguarding Children Board for their combined area (and where they do so, any reference in this section and sections 32 to 34 to the authority establishing the Board shall be read as a reference to the authorities establishing it).

32 Functions and procedure of LSCBs in Wales

(1) The objective of a Local Safeguarding Children Board established under section 31 is—

(a) to co-ordinate what is done by each person or body represented on the Board for the purposes of safeguarding and promoting the welfare of children in the area of the authority by which it is established; and

(b) to ensure the effectiveness of what is done by each such person or body for those purposes.

(2) A Local Safeguarding Children Board established under section 31 is to have such functions in relation to its objective as the Assembly may by regulations prescribe (which may in particular include functions of review or investigation).

(3) The Assembly may by regulations make provision as to the procedures to be followed by a Local Safeguarding Children Board established under section 31.

33 Funding of LSCBs in Wales

(1) Any person or body specified in subsection (3) may make payments towards expenditure incurred by, or for purposes connected with, a Local Safeguarding Children Board established under section 31—

(a) by making the payments directly; or

(b) by contributing to a fund out of which the payments may be made.

(2) Any person or body specified in subsection (3) may provide staff, goods, services, accommodation or other resources for purposes connected with a Local Safeguarding Children Board established under section 31.

(3) The persons and bodies referred to in subsections (1) and (2) are—

(a) the children's services authority in Wales by which the Board is established;

(b) any person who is a Board partner of the authority under section 31(3)(a) to (e);

(c) in a case where the governor of a secure training centre or prison is a Board partner of the authority, the Secretary of State; and

(d) in a case where the director of a contracted out secure training centre or prison is a Board partner of the authority, the contractor.

34 LSCBs in Wales: supplementary

(1) The Assembly may by regulations make provision as to the functions of children's services authorities in Wales relating to Local Safeguarding Children Boards established by them.

(2) A children's services authority in Wales and each of their Board partners must, in exercising their functions relating to a Local Safeguarding Children Board, have regard to any guidance given to them for the purpose by the Assembly.

(3) The Assembly must obtain the consent of the Secretary of State before giving guidance under subsection (2) at any time after the coming into force of any of paragraphs (a) to (c), (f) or (g) of section 31(3).

PART 4

ADVISORY AND SUPPORT SERVICES FOR FAMILY PROCEEDINGS

CAFCASS functions in Wales

35 Functions of the Assembly relating to family proceedings

(1) In respect of family proceedings in which the welfare of children ordinarily resident in Wales is or may be in question, it is a function of the Assembly to—

- (a) safeguard and promote the welfare of the children;
- (b) give advice to any court about any application made to it in such proceedings;
- (c) make provision for the children to be represented in such proceedings;
- (d) provide information, advice and other support for the children and their families.

(2) The Assembly must also make provision for the performance of the functions conferred on Welsh family proceedings officers by virtue of any enactment (whether or not they are exercisable for the purposes of subsection (1)).

(3) In subsection (1), "family proceedings" has the meaning given by section 12 of the Criminal Justice and Court Services Act 2000 (c. 43).

(4) In this Part, "Welsh family proceedings officer" means—

- (a) any member of the staff of the Assembly appointed to exercise the functions of a Welsh family proceedings officer; and
- (b) any other individual exercising functions of a Welsh family proceedings officer by virtue of section 36(2) or (4).

36 Ancillary powers of the Assembly

(1) The Assembly may make arrangements with organisations under which the organisations perform the functions of the Assembly under section 35 on its behalf.

(2) Arrangements under subsection (1) may provide for the organisations to designate individuals who may perform functions of Welsh family proceedings officers.

(3) The Assembly may only make an arrangement under subsection (1) if it is of the opinion—

- (a) that the functions in question will be performed efficiently and to the required standard; and
- (b) that the arrangement represents good value for money.

(4) The Assembly may make arrangements with individuals under which they may perform functions of Welsh family proceedings officers.

(5) The Assembly may make arrangements with an organisation or individual under which staff of the Assembly engaged in the exercise of its functions under section 35 may work for the organisation or individual.

(6) The Assembly may make arrangements with an organisation or individual under which any services provided by the Assembly's staff to the Assembly in the exercise of its functions under section 35 are also made available to the organisation or individual.

(7) The Assembly may charge for anything done under arrangements under subsection (5) and (6).

(8) In this section, references to organisations include public bodies and private or voluntary organisations.

37 Welsh family proceedings officers

(1) The Assembly may authorise a Welsh family proceedings officer of a description prescribed in regulations made by the Secretary of State—

(a) to conduct litigation in relation to any proceedings in any court,

(b) to exercise a right of audience in any proceedings in any court,

in the exercise of his functions.

(2) A Welsh family proceedings officer exercising a right to conduct litigation by virtue of subsection (1)(a) who would otherwise have such a right by virtue of section 28(2)(a) of the Courts and Legal Services Act 1990 (c. 41) is to be treated as having acquired that right solely by virtue of this section.

(3) A Welsh family proceedings officer exercising a right of audience by virtue of subsection (1)(b) who would otherwise have such a right by virtue of section 27(2)(a) of the Courts and Legal Services Act 1990 is to be treated as having acquired that right solely by virtue of this section.

(4) A Welsh family proceedings officer may, subject to rules of court, be cross-examined in any proceedings to the same extent as any witness.

(5) But a Welsh family proceedings officer may not be cross-examined merely because he is exercising a right to conduct litigation or a right of audience granted in accordance with this section.

(6) In this section, "right to conduct litigation" and "right of audience" have the same meanings as in section 119 of the Courts and Legal Services Act 1990.

38 Inspections

(1) Her Majesty's Inspectorate of Court Administration must at the request of the Assembly inspect, and report to the Assembly on—

(a) the discharge by the Assembly of its functions under this Part; and

(b) the discharge by Welsh family proceedings officers of their functions under this Part and any other enactment.

(2) The Assembly may only make a request under subsection (1) with the consent of the Secretary of State.

39 Protection of children

(1) The Protection of Children Act 1999 (c. 14) ("the 1999 Act") shall have effect as if the Assembly, in performing its functions under sections 35 and 36, were a child care organisation within the meaning of that Act.

(2) Arrangements which the Assembly makes with an organisation under section 36(1) must provide that, before selecting an individual to be employed under the arrangements in a child care position, the organisation—

(a) must ascertain whether the individual is included in any of the lists mentioned in section 7(1) of the 1999 Act, and

(b) if he is included in any of those lists, must not select him for that employment.

(3) Such arrangements must provide that, if at any time the organisation has power to refer an individual who is or has been employed in a child care position under the arrangements to the Secretary of State under section 2 of the 1999 Act (inclusion in list on reference following disciplinary actions etc), the organisation must so refer him.

(4) In this section, "child care position" and "employment" have the same meanings as in the 1999 Act.

40 Advisory and support services for family proceedings: supplementary

Schedule 3 (which makes supplementary and consequential provision relating to this Part, including provision relating to functions of Welsh family proceedings officers) has effect.

41 Sharing of information

(1) The Assembly and the Children and Family Court Advisory and Support Service may provide any information to each other for the purposes of their respective functions under this Part and Part 1 of the Criminal Justice and Court Services Act 2000 (c. 43).

(2) A Welsh family proceedings officer and an officer of the Service (within the meaning given by section 11(3) of that Act) may provide any information to each other for the purposes of any of their respective functions.

Transfers

42 Transfer of property from CAFCASS to Assembly

(1) For the purposes of the exercise of functions conferred on the Assembly by or under this Part, the Assembly and the Secretary of State may jointly by order make one or more schemes for the transfer to the Assembly of property, rights and liabilities of the Children and Family Court Advisory and Support Service (in this section, "CAFCASS").

(2) The reference in subsection (1) to rights and liabilities does not include rights and liabilities under a contract of employment.

(3) A scheme under this section may—

(a) specify the property, rights and liabilities to be transferred by the scheme; or

(b) provide for the determination, in accordance with the scheme, of the property, rights and liabilities to be transferred by the scheme.

(4) A scheme under this section may include provision for the creation of rights, or the imposition of liabilities, in relation to property transferred by the scheme.

(5) A scheme under this section has effect in relation to any property, rights and liabilities to which it applies despite any provision (of whatever nature) which would otherwise prevent, penalise or restrict their transfer.

(6) A right of pre-emption or reverter or other similar right does not operate or become exercisable as a result of any transfer under a scheme under this section; and in the case of such a transfer, any such right has effect as if the Assembly were the same person in law as CAFCASS and as if the transfer had not taken place.

(7) The Assembly is to pay such compensation as is just to any person in respect of any right which would, apart from subsections (5) and (6), have operated in favour of, or become exercisable by, that person but which, in consequence of the operation of those subsections, cannot subsequently operate in his favour or become exercisable by him.

(8) A scheme under this section may provide for the determination of any disputes as to whether and, if so, how much compensation is payable under subsection (7).

(9) Subsections (5) to (8) apply in relation to the creation of rights in relation to property as they apply in relation to a transfer of property.

(10) A certificate issued by the Secretary of State and the Assembly jointly that any property, rights or liabilities have or have not been transferred by a scheme under this section is conclusive evidence as to whether they have or have not been so transferred.

43 Transfer of staff from CAFCASS to Assembly

(1) For the purpose of the exercise of functions conferred on the Assembly by or under this Part, the Assembly and the Secretary of State may jointly by order make one or more schemes for the transfer of employees of CAFCASS to the Assembly.

(2) A scheme under this section may apply—

- (a) to any description of employees of CAFCASS;
- (b) to any individual employee of CAFCASS.

(3) A contract of employment of an employee transferred under a scheme under this section—

- (a) is not terminated by the transfer; and
- (b) has effect from the date of the transfer under the scheme as if originally made between the employee and the Assembly.

(4) Where an employee is so transferred—

- (a) all the rights, powers, duties and liabilities of CAFCASS under or in connection with the contract of employment are by virtue of this subsection transferred to the Assembly on the date of the transfer under the scheme; and
- (b) anything done before that date by or in relation to CAFCASS in respect of that contract or the employee is to be treated from that date as having been done by or in relation to the Assembly.

This subsection does not prejudice the generality of subsection (3).

(5) But if the employee informs the Assembly or CAFCASS that he objects to the transfer—

- (a) subsections (3) and (4) do not apply; and

(b) his contract of employment is terminated immediately before the date of transfer but the employee is not to be treated, for any reason, as having been dismissed by CAFCASS.

(6) This section does not prejudice any right of an employee to terminate his contract of employment if (apart from the change of employer) a substantial change is made to his detriment in his working conditions.

(7) A scheme may be made under this section only if any requirements about consultation prescribed in regulations made by the Secretary of State and the Assembly jointly have been complied with in relation to each of the employees of CAFCASS to be transferred under the scheme.

(8) In this section "CAFCASS" has the same meaning as in section 42.

PART 5

MISCELLANEOUS

Private fostering

44 Amendments to notification scheme

(1) Section 67 of the Children Act 1989 (c. 41) (welfare of privately fostered children) is amended as specified in subsections (2) to (6).

(2) In subsection (1)—

(a) after "who are" insert "or are proposed to be";

(b) after "is being" insert "or will be";

(c) for "caring for" substitute "concerned with".

(3) After subsection (2) insert—

"(2A) Regulations under subsection (2)(b) may impose requirements as to the action to be taken by a local authority for the purposes of discharging their duty under subsection (1) where they have received notification of a proposal that a child be privately fostered."

(4) In subsection (3) for "to visit privately fostered children" substitute "for the purpose".

(5) In subsection (5)—

(a) after "child who is" insert "or is proposed to be";

(b) after "is being" insert "or will be".

(6) After subsection (5) insert—

"(6) The Secretary of State may make regulations requiring a local authority to monitor the way in which the authority discharge their functions under this Part (and the regulations may in particular require the authority to appoint an officer for that purpose)."

(7) In Schedule 8 to that Act (privately fostered children) after paragraph 7 insert—

"7A Every local authority must promote public awareness in their area of requirements as to notification for which provision is made under paragraph 7."

(8) The reference to that Act in Schedule 1 to the National Assembly for Wales (Transfer of Functions) Order 1999 (S.I. 1999/672) is to be treated as referring to that Act as amended by this section.

45 Power to establish registration scheme in England

(1) The Secretary of State may by regulations require any person who fosters a child privately in the area of a children's services authority in England to be registered for private fostering by that authority in accordance with the regulations.

(2) Regulations under this section may make supplementary provision relating to the registration of persons for private fostering, including provision as to—

(a) how a person applies for registration and the procedure to be followed in considering an application;

(b) the requirements to be satisfied before a person may be registered;

(c) the circumstances in which a person is disqualified from being registered;

(d) the circumstances in which an application for registration may or must be granted or refused;

(e) the payment of a fee on the making or granting of an application for registration;

(f) the imposition of conditions on registration and the variation or cancellation of such conditions;

(g) the circumstances in which a person's registration may be, or be regarded as, cancelled;

(h) the making of appeals against any determination of a children's services authority in England in relation to a person's registration;

(i) temporary registration, or circumstances in which a person may be regarded as registered;

(j) requirements to be complied with by a children's services authority in England or a person registered under the regulations.

(3) The provision which may be made under subsection (2)(a) includes provision that any person who, in an application for registration under the regulations, knowingly makes a statement which is false or misleading in a material particular is guilty of an offence and liable on summary conviction to a fine not exceeding level 5 on the standard scale.

(4) The requirements for which provision may be made under subsection (2)(b) include requirements relating to—

(a) the suitability of the applicant to foster children privately;

(b) the suitability of the premises in which it is proposed to foster children privately (including their suitability by reference to any other person living there).

(5) The provision which may be made under subsection (2)(c) includes provision that a person may be disqualified where—

(a) an order of a kind specified in the regulations has been made at any time with respect to him;

(b) an order of a kind so specified has been made at any time with respect to any child who has been in his care;

(c) a requirement of a kind so specified has been imposed at any time with respect to any such child, under or by virtue of any enactment;

(d) he has been convicted of a criminal offence of a kind so specified, or a probation order has been made in respect of him for any such offence or he has been discharged absolutely or conditionally for any such offence;

(e) a prohibition has been imposed on him under any specified enactment;

(f) his rights and powers with respect to a child have at any time been vested in a specified authority under a specified enactment;

(g) he lives in the same household as a person who is himself disqualified from being registered or in a household in which such a person is employed.

(6) The provision which may be made under subsection (2)(c) also includes provision for a children's services authority in England to determine whether a person is or is not to be disqualified.

(7) The conditions for which provision may be made under subsection (2)(f) include conditions relating to—

(a) the maintenance of premises in which children are, or are proposed to be, privately fostered;

(b) any other persons living at such premises.

(8) The provision which may be made under subsection (2)(j) includes—

(a) a requirement that a person registered under the regulations obtain the consent of the children's services authority in England by whom he is registered before privately fostering a child;

(b) provision relating to the giving of such consent (including provision as to the circumstances in which, or conditions subject to which, it may or must be given).

(9) The provision which may be made under subsection (2)(j) also includes—

(a) a requirement for a children's services authority in England to undertake annual inspections in relation to persons registered under the regulations (whether in fact privately fostering children or not); and

(b) provision for the payment of a fee by registered persons in respect of such inspections.

(10) Regulations under this section may—

(a) authorise a children's services authority in England to issue a notice to any person whom they believe to be fostering a child privately in their area without being registered in accordance with the regulations; and

(b) provide that a person who, without reasonable excuse, fosters a child privately without being registered in accordance with the regulations while such a notice is issued in respect of him is guilty of an offence and liable on summary conviction to a fine not exceeding level 5 on the standard scale.

(11) Regulations under this section may provide that a person registered under the regulations who without reasonable excuse contravenes or otherwise fails to comply with any requirement imposed on him in the regulations is guilty of an offence and liable on summary conviction to a fine not exceeding level 5 on the standard scale.

(12) Regulations under this section may provide that a person who fosters a child privately while he is disqualified from being registered is guilty of an offence unless—

(a) he is disqualified by virtue of the fact that he lives in the same household as a person who is himself disqualified from being registered or in a household in which such a person is employed; and

(b) he did not know, and had no reasonable grounds for believing, that that person was so disqualified.

(13) Where regulations under this section make provision under subsection (12), they must provide that a person who is guilty of the offence referred to in that subsection is liable on summary conviction to—

(a) a fine not exceeding level 5 on the standard scale, or

(b) a term of imprisonment not exceeding 51 weeks (or, in the case of an offence committed before the commencement of section 281(5) of the Criminal Justice Act 2003 (c. 44), not exceeding six months), or

(c) both.

(14) Regulations under this section may—

(a) make consequential amendments (including repeals) to sections 67(2) to (6) and 68 to 70 of, and paragraphs 6 to 9 of Schedule 8 to, the Children Act 1989 (c. 41);

(b) amend Schedule 1 to the Local Authority Social Services Act 1970 (c. 42) (social services functions) as to add functions of a children's services authority in England under this section to the functions listed in that Schedule.

(15) Nothing in this section affects the scope of section 66(1).

(16) For the purposes of this section references to a person fostering a child privately have the same meaning as in the Children Act 1989.

46 Power to establish registration scheme in Wales

(1) The Assembly may by regulations require any person who fosters a child privately in the area of a children's services authority in Wales to be registered for private fostering by that authority in accordance with the regulations.

(2) Subsections (2) to (15) of section 45 apply in relation to regulations under this section as they apply in relation to regulations under that section with the substitution for references to a children's services authority in England of references to a children's services authority in Wales.

(3) Subsection (16) of that section applies for the purposes of this section.

47 Expiry of powers in sections 45 and 46

(1) If no regulations have been made under section 45 by the relevant time, that section shall (other than for the purposes of section 46(2) and (3)) cease to have effect at that time.

(2) If no regulations have been made under section 46 by the relevant time, that section shall cease to have effect at that time.

(3) In this section, the relevant time is the end of the period of four years beginning with the day on which this Act is passed.

Child minding and day care

48 Child minding and day care

Schedule 4 (which makes provision amending Part 10A of the Children Act 1989 (c. 41) in relation to child minding and day care) has effect.

Local authority services

49 Payments to foster parents

(1) The appropriate person may by order make provision as to the payments to be made—

(a) by a children's services authority in England or Wales or a person exercising functions on its behalf to a local authority foster parent with whom any child is placed by that authority or person under section 23(2)(a) of the Children Act 1989;

(b) by a voluntary organisation to any person with whom any child is placed by that organisation under section 59(1)(a) of that Act.

(2) In subsection (1)—

"appropriate person" means—

(a) the Secretary of State, in relation to a children's services authority in England;

(b) the Assembly, in relation to a children's services authority in Wales;

"local authority foster parent" and "voluntary organisation" have the same meanings as in the Children Act 1989.

(3) In section 23(2)(a) of the Children Act 1989, at the end insert "(subject to section 49 of the Children Act 2004)".

(4) In section 59(1)(a) of that Act, at the end insert "(subject to section 49 of the Children Act 2004)".

50 Intervention

(1) Section 497A of the Education Act 1996 (c. 56) (power to secure proper performance of a local education authority's functions) applies in relation to—

(a) the relevant functions of a children's services authority in England, and

(b) the relevant functions of a children's services authority in Wales,

as it applies in relation to the functions of a local education authority referred to in subsection (1) of that section.

(2) For the purposes of this section, the relevant functions of a children's services authority in England or Wales are—

(a) functions conferred on or exercisable by the authority which are social services functions, so far as those functions relate to children;

(b) the functions conferred on the authority under sections 23C to 24D of the Children Act 1989 (so far as not falling within paragraph (a)); and

(c) the functions conferred on the authority under sections 10, 12 and 17 above (in the case of a children's services authority in England) or under sections 25, 26 and 29 above (in the case of a children's services authority in Wales).

(3) In subsection (2)(a) "social services functions" has the same meaning as in the the Local Authority Social Services Act 1970 (c. 42).

(4) Sections 497AA and 497B of the Education Act 1996 apply accordingly where powers under section 497A of that Act are exercised in relation to any of the relevant functions of a children's services authority in England or Wales.

(5) In the application of sections 497A(2) to (7), 497AA and 497B of that Act in relation to the relevant functions of a children's services authority in England or Wales, references to the local education authority are to be read as references to the children's services authority in England or Wales.

(6) In subsection (5) of section 497A of that Act, the reference to functions to which that section applies includes (for all purposes) relevant functions of a children's services authority in England or Wales.

51 Inspection of local education authorities

In section 38 of the Education Act 1997 (c. 44) (inspection of LEAs), for subsection (2) substitute—

"(2) An inspection of a local education authority in England under this section shall consist of a review of the way in which the authority are performing any function conferred on them in their capacity as a local education authority, other than a function falling within the remit of the Adult Learning Inspectorate under section 53 of the Learning and Skills Act 2000 (c. 21).

(2A) An inspection of a local education authority in Wales under this section shall consist of a review of the way in which the authority are performing—

(a) any function conferred on them in their capacity as a local education authority; and

(b) the functions conferred on them under sections 25 and 26 so far as relating to education, training or youth support services (within the meaning of section 123 of the Learning and Skills Act 2000)."

52 Duty of local authorities to promote educational achievement

In section 22 of the Children Act 1989 (c. 41) (general duty of local authority in relation to children looked after by them), after subsection (3) insert—

"(3A) The duty of a local authority under subsection (3)(a) to safeguard and promote the welfare of a child looked after by them includes in particular a duty to promote the child's educational achievement."

53 Ascertaining children's wishes

(1) In section 17 of the Children Act 1989 (provision of services to children), after subsection (4) insert—

"(4A) Before determining what (if any) services to provide for a particular child in need in the exercise of functions conferred on them by this section, a local authority shall, so far as is reasonably practicable and consistent with the child's welfare—

(a) ascertain the child's wishes and feelings regarding the provision of those services; and

(b) give due consideration (having regard to his age and understanding) to such wishes and feelings of the child as they have been able to ascertain."

(2) In section 20 of that Act (provision of accommodation for children: general), in subsection (6)(a) and (b), after "wishes" insert "and feelings".

(3) In section 47 of that Act (local authority's duty to investigate), after subsection (5) insert—

"(5A) For the purposes of making a determination under this section as to the action to be taken with respect to a child, a local authority shall, so far as is reasonably practicable and consistent with the child's welfare—

(a) ascertain the child's wishes and feelings regarding the action to be taken with respect to him; and

(b) give due consideration (having regard to his age and understanding) to such wishes and feelings of the child as they have been able to ascertain."

54 Information about individual children

In section 83 of the Children Act 1989 (c. 41) (research and returns of information), after subsection (4) insert—

"(4A) Particulars required to be transmitted under subsection (3) or (4) may include particulars relating to and identifying individual children."

55 Social services committees

(1) Sections 2 to 5 of the Local Authority Social Services Act 1970 (c. 42) (social services committees) shall cease to have effect.

(2) In Schedule 1 to that Act (enactments conferring functions assigned to social services committees), for the heading substitute "SOCIAL SERVICES FUNCTIONS".

(3) In section 63(8) of the Health Services and Public Health Act 1968 (c. 46) (instruction), in paragraph (a) of the definition of "relevant enactments", for the words from "for the time being" to "section 2" substitute "are social services functions within the meaning".

(4) In Schedule 1 to the Local Government and Housing Act 1989 (c. 42) (political balance on committees), in paragraph 4(1), in paragraph (a) of the definition of "ordinary committee", for the words from "the authority's" to "any other committee" substitute "any committee".

(5) In section 102 of the Local Government Act 2000 (c. 22) (social services functions)—

(a) omit subsection (1);

(b) in subsection (2), for "that Act" substitute "the Local Authority Social Services Act 1970".

56 Social services functions

In Schedule 1 to the Local Authority Social Services Act 1970 (c. 42) (functions which are social services functions), at the end insert—

"Children Act 2004	
Sections 13 to 16 and 31 to 34	Functions relating to Local Safeguarding Children Boards."

Other provisions

57 Fees payable to adoption review panel members

In section 12 of the Adoption and Children Act 2002 (c. 38) (independent review of determinations), in subsection (3)(d) (power to make provision as to the payment of expenses of members of a panel) for "expenses of" substitute "fees to".

58 Reasonable punishment

(1) In relation to any offence specified in subsection (2), battery of a child cannot be justified on the ground that it constituted reasonable punishment.

(2) The offences referred to in subsection (1) are—

(a) an offence under section 18 or 20 of the Offences against the Person Act 1861 (c. 100) (wounding and causing grievous bodily harm);

(b) an offence under section 47 of that Act (assault occasioning actual bodily harm);

(c) an offence under section 1 of the Children and Young Persons Act 1933 (c. 12) (cruelty to persons under 16).

(3) Battery of a child causing actual bodily harm to the child cannot be justified in any civil proceedings on the ground that it constituted reasonable punishment.

(4) For the purposes of subsection (3) "actual bodily harm" has the same meaning as it has for the purposes of section 47 of the Offences against the Person Act 1861.

(5) In section 1 of the Children and Young Persons Act 1933, omit subsection (7).

59 Power to give financial assistance

(1) Section 14 of the Education Act 2002 (c. 32) (power of Secretary of State and Assembly to give financial assistance for purposes related to education or childcare) is amended as specified in subsections (2) to (4).

(2) In subsection (2) of that section (purposes for which assistance may be given), at the end insert—

"(j) the promotion of the welfare of children and their parents;

(k) the provision of support for parenting (including support for prospective parents)."

(3) After that subsection insert—

"(2A) In subsection (2)(j), "children" means persons under the age of twenty."

(4) In the heading to that section, for "childcare" substitute "children etc".

(5) In the heading to Part 2 of that Act, for "childcare" substitute "children etc".

60 Child safety orders

(1) The Crime and Disorder Act 1998 (c. 37) is amended as follows.

(2) In section 8(1)(a) (power to make parenting order where a child safety order is made), at the end insert "or the court determines on an application under section 12(6) below that a child has failed to comply with any requirement included in such an order".

(3) In section 11(4) (maximum period permitted for child safety orders), for the words from "three months" to the end substitute "twelve months".

(4) In section 12, omit subsections (6)(a) and (7) (power to make care order on breach of child safety order).

61 Children's Commissioner for Wales: powers of entry

In the Care Standards Act 2000 (c. 14), in section 76 (further functions of Children's Commissioner for Wales), at the end insert—

"(8) The Commissioner or a person authorised by him may for the purposes of any function of the Commissioner under section 72B or 73 or subsection (4) of this section at any reasonable time—

(a) enter any premises, other than a private dwelling, for the purposes of interviewing any child accommodated or cared for there; and

(b) if the child consents, interview the child in private."

62 Publication of material relating to legal proceedings

(1) In section 97(2) of the Children Act 1989 (c. 41) (privacy for children involved in certain proceedings), after "publish" insert "to the public at large or any section of the public".

(2) In section 12(4) of the Administration of Justice Act 1960 (c. 65) (publication of information relating to proceedings in private), at the end insert "(and in particular where the publication is not so punishable by reason of being authorised by rules of court)".

(3) In section 66 of the Adoption Act 1976 (c. 36) (rules of procedure), after subsection (5) insert—

"(5A) Rules may, for the purposes of the law relating to contempt of court, authorise the publication in such circumstances as may be specified of information relating to proceedings held in private involving children."

(4) In section 145(1) of the Magistrates' Courts Act 1980 (c. 43) (rules: supplementary), after paragraph (g) insert—

“(ga) authorising, for the purposes of the law relating to contempt of court, the publication in such circumstances as may be specified of information relating to proceedings referred to in section 12(1)(a) of the Administration of Justice Act 1960 which are held in private;”.

(5) In section 40(4) of the Matrimonial and Family Proceedings Act 1984 (c. 42) (family proceedings rules), in paragraph (a) after “County Courts Act 1984;” insert—

“(aa) authorise, for the purposes of the law relating to contempt of court, the publication in such circumstances as may be specified of information relating to family proceedings held in private;”.

(6) In section 141 of the Adoption and Children Act 2002 (c. 38) (rules of procedure) at the end insert—

“(6) Rules may, for the purposes of the law relating to contempt of court, authorise the publication in such circumstances as may be specified of information relating to proceedings held in private involving children.”

(7) In section 76 of the Courts Act 2003 (c. 39) (Family Procedure Rules: further provision) after subsection (2) insert—

“(2A) Family Procedure Rules may, for the purposes of the law relating to contempt of court, authorise the publication in such circumstances as may be specified of information relating to family proceedings held in private.”

63 Disclosure of information by Inland Revenue

(1) In Schedule 5 to the Tax Credits Act 2002 (c. 21) (use and disclosure of information), after paragraph 10 insert—

“10A Provision of information by Board for purposes relating to welfare of children

10A (1) This paragraph applies to information, other than information relating to a person’s income, which is held for the purposes of functions relating to tax credits, child benefit or guardian’s allowance—

(a) by the Board, or

(b) by a person providing services to the Board, in connection with the provision of those services.

(2) Information to which this paragraph applies may be supplied to—

(a) a local authority in England and Wales for use for the purpose of any enquiry or investigation under Part 5 of the Children Act 1989 relating to the welfare of a child;

(b) a local authority in Scotland for use for the purpose of any enquiry or investigation under Chapter 3 of Part 2 of the Children (Scotland) Act 1995 relating to the welfare of a child;

(c) an authority in Northern Ireland for use for the purpose of any enquiry or investigation under Part 6 of the Children (Northern Ireland) Order 1995 (S.I. 1995/755 (N.I.2)) relating to the welfare of a child.

(3) Information supplied under this paragraph is not to be supplied by the recipient to any other person or body unless it is supplied—

(a) for the purpose of any enquiry or investigation referred to in sub-paragraph (2) above,

(b) for the purpose of civil or criminal proceedings, or

(c) where paragraph (a) or (b) does not apply, to a person to whom the information could be supplied directly by or under the authority of the Board.

(4) Information may not be supplied under sub-paragraph (3)(b) or (c) without the authority of the Board.

(5) A person commits an offence if he discloses information supplied to him under this paragraph unless the disclosure is made—

(a) in accordance with sub-paragraph (3),

(b) in accordance with an enactment or an order of a court,

(c) with consent given by or on behalf of the person to whom the information relates, or

(d) in such a way as to prevent the identification of the person to whom it relates.

(6) It is a defence for a person charged with an offence under sub-paragraph (5) to prove that he reasonably believed that his disclosure was lawful.

(7) A person guilty of an offence under sub-paragraph (5) is liable—

(a) on conviction on indictment, to imprisonment for a term not exceeding two years, to a fine or to both;

(b) on summary conviction in England and Wales, to imprisonment for a term not exceeding twelve months, to a fine not exceeding the statutory maximum or to both;

(c) on summary conviction in Scotland or Northern Ireland, to imprisonment for a term not exceeding six months, to a fine not exceeding the statutory maximum or to both.

(8) In sub-paragraph (2) "child" means a person under the age of eighteen and—

(a) in paragraph (a), "local authority" has the meaning given by section 105(1) of the Children Act 1989;

(b) in paragraph (b), "local authority" has the meaning given by section 93(1) of the Children (Scotland) Act 1995; and

(c) in paragraph (c), "authority" has the meaning given by Article 2 of the Children (Northern Ireland) Order 1995 (S.I. 1995/755 (N.I.2)).

(9) The reference to an enactment in sub-paragraph (5)(b) includes a reference to an enactment comprised in, or in an instrument made under, an Act of the Scottish Parliament."

(2) In relation to an offence committed under sub-paragraph (5) of paragraph 10A of Schedule 5 to the Tax Credits Act 2002 (c. 21) (as inserted by subsection (1) above) before the commencement of section 154 of the Criminal Justice Act 2003, the

reference in sub-paragraph (7)(b) of that paragraph to twelve months shall be read as a reference to six months.

PART 6

GENERAL

64 Repeals

The enactments specified in Schedule 5 are repealed to the extent specified.

65 Interpretation

(1) In this Act—

"the Assembly" means the National Assembly for Wales;

"child" means, subject to section 9, a person under the age of eighteen (and "children" is to be construed accordingly);

"children's services authority in England" means—

(a) a county council in England;

(b) a metropolitan district council;

(c) a non-metropolitan district council for an area for which there is no county council;

(d) a London borough council;

(e) the Common Council of the City of London;

(f) the Council of the Isles of Scilly;

"children's services authority in Wales" means a county council or county borough council in Wales.

(2) This Act applies in relation to the Isles of Scilly subject to such modifications as may be specified by order made by the Secretary of State.

(3) In this Act—

(a) references to a prison include a young offender institution;

(b) references to a contracted out secure training centre, and to the contractor in relation to such a secure training centre, have the meanings given by section 15 of the Criminal Justice and Public Order Act 1994 (c. 33);

(c) references to a contracted out prison, and to the contractor in relation to such a prison, have the meanings given by section 84(4) of the Criminal Justice Act 1991 (c. 53).

(4) Where—

(a) a contract under section 7 of the Criminal Justice and Public Order Act 1994 is for the time being in force in relation to part of a secure training centre, or

(b) a contract under section 84 of the Criminal Justice Act 1991 is for the time being in force in relation to part of a prison,

this Act has effect as if each part of the secure training centre or prison were a separate institution.

66 Regulations and orders

(1) Any power to make regulations or an order under this Act includes power—

(a) to make different provision for different purposes;

(b) to make different provision for different cases or areas;

(c) to make incidental, supplementary, consequential or transitional provision or savings.

(2) Any power to make regulations or an order under this Act, other than an order under section 42 or 43, is exercisable by statutory instrument.

(3) The Secretary of State may not make a statutory instrument containing regulations under section 12 or 45 unless a draft of the instrument has been laid before, and approved by resolution of, each House of Parliament.

(4) The Secretary of State may not make a statutory instrument containing the first order under section 49 unless a draft of the instrument has been laid before, and approved by resolution of, each House of Parliament.

(5) A statutory instrument containing—

(a) any regulations made by the Secretary of State under this Act to which subsection (3) does not apply,

(b) an order made by the Secretary of State under section 49 to which subsection (4) does not apply, or

(c) an order made by the Secretary of State under section 11(1)(d) or section 65(2),

is subject to annulment in pursuance of a resolution of either House of Parliament.

(6) Subsection (5) does not apply to regulations made by the Secretary of State jointly with the Assembly under section 43(7).

67 Commencement

(1) Part 1 comes into force on the day on which this Act is passed.

(2) Part 2 comes into force in accordance with provision made by order by the Secretary of State.

(3) Part 3 comes into force in accordance with provision made by order by the Assembly subject to subsections (4) and (5).

(4) The Assembly must obtain the consent of the Secretary of State before making provision under subsection (3) in relation to section 25(4)(a) to (c) or 31(3)(a) to (c), (f) or (g).

(5) In section 28, the following provisions come into force in accordance with provision made by order by the Secretary of State after consulting the Assembly—

(a) subsection (1)(d) to (h);

(b) subsection (2), so far as relating to the persons and bodies referred to in subsection (1)(d) to (h);

(c) subsection (5).

(6) Part 4 comes into force in accordance with provision made by order by the Assembly with the consent of the Secretary of State.

(7) In Part 5—

(a) section 44 so far as relating to England comes into force in accordance with provision made by order by the Secretary of State, and so far as relating to Wales in accordance with provision made by order by the Assembly;

(b) sections 45 to 47 come into force at the end of the period of two months beginning with the day on which this Act is passed;

(c) section 48 and Schedule 4 so far as relating to England come into force in accordance with provision made by order by the Secretary of State, and so far as relating to Wales in accordance with provision made by order by the Assembly;

(d) section 49 comes into force at the end of the period of two months beginning with the day on which this Act is passed;

(e) sections 50 to 57 so far as relating to England come into force in accordance with provision made by order by the Secretary of State, and so far as relating to Wales in accordance with provision made by order by the Assembly;

(f) section 58 comes into force at the end of the period of two months beginning with the day on which this Act is passed;

(g) section 59 comes into force on the day on which this Act is passed;

(h) section 60 comes into force in accordance with provision made by order by the Secretary of State;

(i) section 61 comes into force in accordance with provision made by order by the Assembly;

(j) section 62 comes into force in accordance with provision made by order by the Lord Chancellor;

(k) section 63 comes into force on the day on which this Act is passed.

(8) This Part comes into force on the day on which this Act is passed except that Schedule 5 comes into force in accordance with the commencement provisions set out in that Schedule.

68 Extent

(1) Part 1 extends to the whole of the United Kingdom (unless otherwise specifically provided).

(2) Parts 2 to 4 extend to England and Wales only.

(3) In Part 5—

(a) sections 44 to 62 extend to England and Wales only;

(b) section 63 extends to the whole of the United Kingdom.

(4) In this Part—

(a) section 64 and Schedule 5 extend to England and Wales only; and

(b) the remaining provisions extend to the whole of the United Kingdom.

69 Short title

This Act may be cited as the Children Act 2004.

SCHEDULES

SCHEDULE 1

Section 1

CHILDREN'S COMMISSIONER

Status

1 (1) The Children's Commissioner is to be a corporation sole.

(2) The Children's Commissioner is not to be regarded as the servant or agent of the Crown or as enjoying any status, immunity or privilege of the Crown; and his property is not to be regarded as property of, or property held on behalf of, the Crown.

General powers

2 (1) The Children's Commissioner may do anything which appears to him to be necessary or expedient for the purpose of, or in connection with, the exercise of his functions.

(2) In particular he may—

(a) co-operate with other public authorities in the United Kingdom;

(b) enter into contracts; and

(c) acquire, hold and dispose of any property.

Appointment and tenure of office

3 (1) The Children's Commissioner is to be appointed by the Secretary of State.

(2) The Secretary of State must, to such extent and in such manner as he thinks fit, involve children in the appointment of the Children's Commissioner.

(3) Subject to the provisions of this paragraph, a person shall hold and vacate office as the Children's Commissioner in accordance with the terms and conditions of his appointment as determined by the Secretary of State.

(4) An appointment as the Children's Commissioner shall be for a term not exceeding five years.

(5) A person who has held office as the Children's Commissioner is eligible for reappointment once only.

(6) The Children's Commissioner may at any time resign by notice in writing to the Secretary of State.

(7) The Secretary of State may remove the Children's Commissioner from office if he is satisfied that he has—

(a) become unfit or unable properly to discharge his functions; or

(b) behaved in a way that is not compatible with his continuing in office.

Remuneration

4 The Secretary of State must—

(a) pay the Children's Commissioner such remuneration and allowances, and
(b) pay or make provision for the payment of such pension or gratuities to or in respect of him,

as may be provided under the terms of his appointment.

Staff

5 (1) The Children's Commissioner may appoint any staff he considers necessary for assisting him in the exercise of his functions, one of whom shall be appointed as deputy Children's Commissioner.

(2) During any vacancy in the office of Children's Commissioner or at any time when the Children's Commissioner is for any reason unable to act, the deputy Children's Commissioner shall exercise his functions (and any property or rights vested in the Children's Commissioner may accordingly be dealt with by the deputy Children's Commissioner as if vested in him).

(3) Without prejudice to sub-paragraph (2), any member of the Children's Commissioner's staff may, so far as authorised by him, exercise any of his functions.

Pensions

6 (1) In the Superannuation Act 1972 (c. 11), in Schedule 1 (kinds of employment etc to which section 1 of that Act applies)—

(a) in the list of "Other Bodies", at the end insert "Employment by the Children's Commissioner";
(b) in the list of "Offices", at the appropriate place insert "Children's Commissioner".

(2) The Secretary of State must pay to the Minister for the Civil Service, at such times as the Minister may direct, such sums as he may determine in respect of any increase attributable to sub-paragraph (1) in the sums payable out of money provided by Parliament under the Superannuation Act 1972.

Funding

7 The Secretary of State may make payments to the Children's Commissioner of such amounts, at such times and on such conditions (if any) as the Secretary of State considers appropriate.

Accounts

8 (1) The Children's Commissioner must—

(a) keep proper accounting records;
(b) prepare a statement of accounts for each financial year; and
(c) send a copy of each such statement of accounts to the Secretary of State and the Comptroller and Auditor General as soon as possible after the end of the financial year to which the statement relates.

(2) The Comptroller and Auditor General must examine, certify and report on each statement of accounts sent to him under sub-paragraph (1)(c) and must lay copies of the statement and of his report before Parliament.

(3) In this paragraph, "financial year" means—

(a) the period beginning with the date on which the first Children's Commissioner is appointed and ending with 31st March next following that date; and

(b) each successive period of twelve months ending with 31st March.

Evidence

9 (1) A document purporting to be duly executed under the seal of the Children's Commissioner or to be signed by him or on his behalf is to be received in evidence and, unless the contrary is proved, taken to be so executed or signed.

(2) This paragraph does not extend to Scotland.

Protection from defamation actions

10 For the purposes of the law of defamation—

(a) any statement made by the Children's Commissioner in a report published under this Part has absolute privilege; and

(b) any other statement made by the Children's Commissioner or a member of his staff for the purposes of this Part has qualified privilege.

Regulated position

11 In the Criminal Justice and Court Services Act 2000 (c. 43), in section 36(6) (meaning of "regulated position"), after paragraph (f) insert—

"(fa) Children's Commissioner and deputy Children's Commissioner appointed under Part 1 of the Children Act 2004,".

Disqualifications

12 In the House of Commons Disqualification Act 1975 (c. 24), in Part 3 of Schedule 1 (certain disqualifying offices), at the appropriate places insert the following entries—

"Children's Commissioner";

"Member of staff of the Children's Commissioner".

13 In the Northern Ireland Assembly Disqualification Act 1975 (c. 25), in Part 3 of Schedule 1 (certain disqualifying offices), at the appropriate places insert the following entries—

"Children's Commissioner";

"Member of staff of the Children's Commissioner".

SCHEDULE 2

Section 18

DIRECTOR OF CHILDREN'S SERVICES: CONSEQUENTIAL AMENDMENTS

Children and Young Persons Act 1933 (c. 12)

1 In section 96 of the Children and Young Persons Act 1933 (provisions as to local authorities), in subsection (8), for "or the chief education officer of the authority" substitute "of the authority, the director of children's services (in the case of an authority in England) or the chief education officer (in the case of an authority in Wales)".

Local Authority Social Services Act 1970 (c. 42)

2 (1) The Local Authority Social Services Act 1970 is amended as follows.

(2) In section 6 (director of social services)—

(a) before subsection (1) insert—

"(A1) A local authority in England shall appoint an officer, to be known as the director of adult social services, for the purposes of their social services functions, other than those for which the authority's director of children's services is responsible under section 18 of the Children Act 2004.";

(b) in subsection (1), after "local authority" insert "in Wales";

(c) in subsection (2), after "director of", in both places, insert "adult social services or (as the case may be)";

(d) in subsection (6), for "a director of social services" substitute "a person under this section".

(3) In Schedule 1, in the entry for "Sections 6 and 7B of this Act", after the words "Appointment of" insert "director of adult social services or".

Local Government and Housing Act 1989 (c. 42)

3 In section 2 of the Local Government and Housing Act 1989 (politically restricted posts), in subsection (6)—

(a) after "means—" insert—

"(za) the director of children's services appointed under section 18 of the Children Act 2004 and the director of adult social services appointed under section 6(A1) of the Local Authority Social Services Act 1970 (in the case of a local authority in England);";

(b) in paragraph (a), at the end insert "(in the case of a local authority in Wales)";

(c) in paragraph (c) after "director of social services" insert "(in the case of a local authority in Wales)".

Education Act 1996 (c. 56)

4 (1) The Education Act 1996 is amended as follows.

(2) In section 532 (appointment of chief education officer), for "A local authority's duties" substitute "The duties of a local education authority in Wales".

(3) In section 566 (evidence: documents), in subsection (1)(a), for "chief education officer of that authority" substitute "director of children's services (in the case of an authority in England) or the chief education officer (in the case of an authority in Wales)".

Crime and Disorder Act 1998 (c. 37)

5 (1) The Crime and Disorder Act 1998 is amended as follows.

(2) In section 8 (responsible officers in relation to parenting orders), in subsection (8)(bb), after "nominated by" insert "a person appointed as director of children's services under section 18 of the Children Act 2004 or by".

(3) In section 39 (youth offending teams), in subsection (5)—

(a) after paragraph (a) insert—

"(aa) where the local authority is in England, a person with experience of social work in relation to children nominated by the director of children's services appointed by the local authority under section 18 of the Children Act 2004;";

(b) in paragraph (b) for "a social worker of a" substitute "where the local authority is in Wales, a social worker of the";

(c) after paragraph (d) insert—

"(da) where the local authority is in England, a person with experience in education nominated by the director of children's services appointed by the local authority under section 18 of the Children Act 2004;";

(d) in paragraph (e) insert at the beginning "where the local authority is in Wales,".

Protection of Children Act 1999 (c. 14)

6 In section 4C of the Protection of Children Act 1999 (restoration to the list) in subsection (1), for "director of social services of a local authority" substitute "director of children's services of a local authority in England or a director of social services of a local authority in Wales".

Criminal Justice and Court Services Act 2000 (c. 43)

7 (1) The Criminal Justice and Court Services Act 2000 is amended as follows.

(2) In section 34 (restoration of disqualification order), in subsection (1), for "a director of social services of a local authority" substitute "a director of children's services of a local authority in England or a director of social services of a local authority in Wales".

(3) In section 36 (meaning of "regulated position"), in subsection (6)—

(a) after paragraph (b) insert—

"(ba) director of children's services and director of adult social services of a local authority in England,";

(b) in paragraph (c) at the end insert "in Wales";
(c) in paragraph (d) at the end insert "in Wales".

Criminal Justice Act 2003 (c. 44)

8 In section 322 of the Criminal Justice Act 2003 (individual support orders), in the new section 1AA to be inserted in the Crime and Disorder Act 1998 (c. 37), in subsection (10)(b), after "nominated by" insert "a person appointed as director of children's services under section 18 of the Children Act 2004 or by".

SCHEDULE 3

Section 40

ADVISORY AND SUPPORT SERVICES FOR FAMILY PROCEEDINGS

Domestic Proceedings and Magistrates' Courts Act 1978 (c. 22)

1 In section 26 of the Domestic Proceedings and Magistrates' Courts Act 1978 (reconciliation), in subsection (2), after "Criminal Justice and Court Services Act 2000)" insert ", a Welsh family proceedings officer (within the meaning given by section 35 of the Children Act 2004)".

Child Abduction and Custody Act 1985 (c. 60)

2 The Child Abduction and Custody Act 1985 is amended as follows.

3 In sections 6(a) and 21(a) (reports), after "an officer of the Service" insert "or a Welsh family proceedings officer".

4 In section 27 (interpretation), after subsection (5) insert—

"(5A) In this Act "Welsh family proceedings officer" has the meaning given by section 35 of the Children Act 2004".

Children Act 1989 (c. 41)

5 The Children Act 1989 is amended as follows.

6 In section 7 (welfare reports), in subsections (1)(a) and (b) and (5), after "an officer of the Service" insert "or a Welsh family proceedings officer".

7 In section 16 (family assistance orders), in subsection (1), after "an officer of the Service" insert "or a Welsh family proceedings officer".

8 (1) Section 26 (review of cases etc) is amended as follows.

(2) In subsection (2A)(c) after "Service" insert "or a Welsh family proceedings officer".

(3) After subsection (2C) insert—

"(2D) The power to make regulations in subsection (2C) is exercisable in relation to functions of Welsh family proceedings officers only with the consent of the National Assembly for Wales."

9 (1) Section 41 (representation of child) is amended as follows.

(2) In subsection (1), after "an officer of the Service" insert "or a Welsh family proceedings officer".

(3) In subsections (2) and (4)(a), after "officer of the Service" insert "or Welsh family proceedings officer".

(4) In subsection (10)—

(a) in paragraphs (a) and (b), after "officer of the Service" insert "or Welsh family proceedings officer";

(b) in paragraph (c), after "officers of the Service" insert "or Welsh family proceedings officers".

(5) In subsection (11), after "an officer of the Service" insert "or a Welsh family proceedings officer".

10 In section 42 (rights of officers of the Service), in subsections (1) and (2), after "an officer of the Service" insert "or Welsh family proceedings officer".

11 In section 105(1) (interpretation), at the end insert—

""Welsh family proceedings officer" has the meaning given by section 35 of the Children Act 2004."

Criminal Justice and Court Services Act 2000 (c. 43)

12 The Criminal Justice and Court Services Act 2000 is amended as follows.

13 In section 12 (principal functions of CAFCASS), in subsection (1), after "the welfare of children" insert "other than children ordinarily resident in Wales".

14 In paragraph 1 of Schedule 2 (members of CAFCASS), for "ten" substitute "nine".

Adoption and Children Act 2002 (c. 38)

15 The Adoption and Children Act 2002 is amended as follows.

16 (1) Section 102 (officers of the Service) is amended as follows.

(2) In subsection (1), at the end insert "or a Welsh family proceedings officer".

(3) In subsection (7), after "officer of the Service" insert "or a Welsh family proceedings officer".

(4) After that subsection insert—

"(8) In this section and section 103 "Welsh family proceedings officer" has the meaning given by section 35 of the Children Act 2004."

17 In section 103 (rights of officers of the Service), in subsections (1) and (2), after "officer of the Service" insert "or a Welsh family proceedings officer".

Sexual Offences Act 2003 (c. 42)

18 In section 21 of the Sexual Offences Act 2003 (positions of trust), in subsection (12)(a), after "officer of the Service" insert "or Welsh family proceedings officer (within the meaning given by section 35 of the Children Act 2004)".

SCHEDULE 4

Section 48

CHILD MINDING AND DAY CARE

1 Part 10A of the Children Act 1989 (c. 41) is amended as follows.

Amendments relating to child minding and day care

Conditions imposed by justice of the peace or tribunal

2 (1) In section 79B(3)(d) and (4)(d), for "by the registration authority" substitute "under this Part".

(2) In section 79G(2), omit "under section 79F(3)".

Application fees

3 (1) In section 79E(2), at the end insert—

"(c) be accompanied by the prescribed fee."

(2) In section 79F(1) and (2)—

(a) after "on an application" insert "under section 79E";

(b) omit paragraph (b) and the preceding "and".

Fees payable by registered persons

4 (1) In section 79G(1), for "an annual fee" substitute "a fee".

(2) In Schedule 9A—

(a) in the heading before paragraph 7, omit "Annual";

(b) in paragraph 7, for the words from "at prescribed times" to the end substitute ", at or by the prescribed times, fees of the prescribed amounts in respect of the discharge by the registration authority of its functions under Part XA."

Waiver of disqualification

5 In Schedule 9A, in paragraph 4(3A)—

(a) after "disqualified for registration" insert "(and may in particular provide for a person not to be disqualified for registration for the purposes of sub-paragraphs (4) and (5))";

(b) in paragraph (b), omit "to his registration".

Amendments relating to day care only

Qualification for registration

6 In section 79B(4)—

(a) for paragraphs (a) and (b) substitute—

"(a) he has made adequate arrangements to ensure that—

(i) every person (other than himself and the responsible individual) looking after children on the premises is suitable to look after children under the age of eight; and

(ii) every person (other than himself and the responsible individual) living or working on the premises is suitable to be in regular contact with children under the age of eight;

(b) the responsible individual—

(i) is suitable to look after children under the age of eight, or

(ii) if he is not looking after such children, is suitable to be in regular contact with them;";

(b) in subsection (5), for "(4)(b)" substitute "(4)(a)";

(c) after subsection (5) insert—

"(5ZA) For the purposes of subsection (4), "the responsible individual" means—

(a) in a case of one individual working on the premises in the provision of day care, that person;

(b) in a case of two or more individuals so working, the individual so working who is in charge."

Hotels etc

7 In Schedule 9A, after paragraph 2 insert—

"2A (1) Part XA does not apply to provision of day care in a hotel, guest house or other similar establishment for children staying in that establishment where—

(a) the provision takes place only between 6 pm and 2 am; and

(b) the person providing the care is doing so for no more than two different clients at the same time.

(2) For the purposes of sub-paragraph (1)(b), a "client" is a person at whose request (or persons at whose joint request) day care is provided for a child."

Prohibition in respect of disqualified persons

8 In Schedule 9A, in paragraph 4(4)—

(a) after "or be" insert "directly";

(b) omit ", or have any financial interest in,".

Unincorporated associations

9 In Schedule 9A, after paragraph 5 insert—

"5A Provision of day care: unincorporated associations

5A (1) References in Part XA to a person, so far as relating to the provision of day care, include an unincorporated association.

(2) Proceedings for an offence under Part XA which is alleged to have been committed by an unincorporated association must be brought in the name of the association (and not in that of any of its members).

(3) For the purpose of any such proceedings, rules of court relating to the service of documents are to have effect as if the association were a body corporate.

(4) In proceedings for an offence under Part XA brought against an unincorporated association, section 33 of the Criminal Justice Act 1925 and Schedule 3 to the Magistrates' Courts Act 1980 (procedure) apply as they do in relation to a body corporate.

(5) A fine imposed on an unincorporated association on its conviction of an offence under Part XA is to be paid out of the funds of the association.

(6) If an offence under Part XA committed by an unincorporated association is shown—

(a) to have been committed with the consent or connivance of an officer of the association or a member of its governing body, or

(b) to be attributable to any neglect on the part of such an officer or member,

the officer or member as well as the association is guilty of the offence and liable to proceeded against and punished accordingly."

SCHEDULE 5

Section 64

REPEALS

PART 1

PLANS

Short title and chapter	*Extent of repeal*
Children Act 1989 (c. 41)	In Schedule 2, paragraph 1A.
Education Act 1996 (c. 56)	Section 527A.
Education Act 1997 (c. 44)	Section 9.
School Standards and Framework Act 1998 (c. 31)	Section 2.
	Sections 6 and 7.
	Sections 26 to 26B.
	In section 27(2), the words "section 26,".
	Section 119(5)(b) and the preceding "and".

These repeals come into force—

(a) so far as relating to England, in accordance with provision made by order by the Secretary of State;

(b) so far as relating to Wales, in accordance with provision so made by the Assembly.

Short title and chapter	*Extent of repeal*
	Sections 120 and 121.
	In Schedule 6— (a) paragraph 3(4)(b) and the preceding "and"; (b) paragraph 8(4).
	In Schedule 30, paragraph 144.
Learning and Skills Act 2000 (c. 21)	In Schedule 7— (a) paragraph 35(2)(b); (b) paragraph 42(2)(a).
	In Schedule 9, paragraphs 80 and 81.
Adoption and Children Act 2002 (c. 38)	Section 5.
Education Act 2002 (c. 32)	In section 150— (a) subsections (2) to (4); (b) in subsection (5), the words from "and early years development plans" to "childcare plans"".

These repeals come into force—
(a) so far as relating to England, in accordance with provision made by order by the Secretary of State;
(b) so far as relating to Wales, in accordance with provision so made by the Assembly.

PART 2

CHILD MINDING AND DAY CARE

Short title and chapter	*Extent of repeal*
Children Act 1989 (c. 41)	In section 79F(1) and (2), paragraph (b) and the preceding "and".
	In section 79G(2), the words "under section 79F(3)".
	In Schedule 9A— (a) in paragraph 4(3A)(b), the words "to his registration"; (b) in paragraph 4(4), the words ", or have any financial interest in,"; (c) in the heading before paragraph 7, the word "Annual".

These repeals come into force—
(a) so far as relating to England, in accordance with provision made by order by the Secretary of State;
(b) so far as relating to Wales, in accordance with provision so made by the Assembly.

PART 3

INSPECTION OF LOCAL EDUCATION AUTHORITIES

Short title and chapter	*Extent of repeal*
Disability Discrimination Act 1995 (c. 50)	Section 28D(6).

This repeal comes into force—
(a) so far as relating to England, in accordance with provision made by order by the Secretary of State;
(b) so far as relating to Wales, in accordance with provision so made by the Assembly.

PART 4

SOCIAL SERVICES COMMITTEES AND DEPARTMENTS

Short title and chapter	*Extent of repeal*
Children and Young Persons Act 1933 (c. 12)	In section 96(7), the words from "Subject to" to "that committee)".
Children and Young Persons Act 1963 (c. 37)	In section 56(2)— (a) the words "and subsection (1) of section 3 of the Local Authority Social Services Act 1970"; (b) the words "and section 2 of the said Act of 1970 respectively".
Local Authority Social Services Act 1970 (c. 42)	Sections 2 to 5.
Local Government Act 1972 (c. 70)	Section 101(9)(f).
Mental Health Act 1983 (c. 20)	In section 14, the words "of their social services department".
Police and Criminal Evidence Act 1984 (c. 60)	In section 63B(10), in the definition of "appropriate adult", the words "social services department".
Local Government and Housing Act 1989 (c. 42)	Section 13(2)(c). In Schedule 1, in paragraph 4(2)— (a) in paragraph (a) of the definition of "ordinary sub-committee", the words from "of the authority's" to "any other sub-committee"; and (b) the definition of "social services committee".
Criminal Justice Act 1991 (c. 53)	In sections 43(5) and 65(1)(b) and (1B)(a), the words "social services department".

These repeals come into force—
(a) so far as relating to England, in accordance with provision made by order by the Secretary of State;
(b) so far as relating to Wales, in accordance with provision so made by the Assembly.

Short title and chapter	*Extent of repeal*
Crime (Sentences) Act 1997 (c. 43)	In section 31(2A)(b), the words "social services department of the". In Schedule 1, in the table in paragraph 9(6), the words "social services department".
Crime and Disorder Act 1998 (c. 37)	The words "social services department" in— (a) section 1AA(9) and (10)(a); (b) section 8(8)(b); (c) section 9(2B)(b); (d) section 11(8)(a); (e) section 18(4)(a); (f) section 39(5)(b); (g) section 65(7)(b); (h) section 98(3) (in the words substituted by that provision).
Powers of Criminal Courts (Sentencing) Act 2000 (c. 6)	The words "social services department" in— (a) section 46(5)(a) and (b); (b) section 69(4)(b), (6)(a) and (10)(a); (c) section 73(5); (d) section 74(5)(b) and (7)(a); (e) section 103(3)(b) and (5)(a); (f) section 162(2)(a) and (b).
Local Government Act 2000 (c. 22)	Section 102(1).
Criminal Justice and Court Services Act 2000 (c. 43)	In section 64(6), in the definition of "appropriate adult", the words "social services department".
Criminal Justice Act 2003 (c. 44)	The words "social services department" in— (a) section 158(2)(b); (b) section 161(8)(b); (c) section 199(4)(b); (d) paragraph 5(4) of Schedule 38 (in the words substituted by that provision).

These repeals come into force—
(a) so far as relating to England, in accordance with provision made by order by the Secretary of State;
(b) so far as relating to Wales, in accordance with provision so made by the Assembly.

PART 5

REASONABLE PUNISHMENT

Short title and chapter	*Extent of repeal*
Children and Young Persons Act 1933 (c. 12)	Section 1(7).

This repeal comes into force at the same time as section 58.

PART 6

CHILD SAFETY ORDERS

Short title and chapter	*Extent of repeal*
Crime and Disorder Act 1998 (c. 37)	Section 12(6)(a) and (7).
These repeals come into force at the same time as section 60.	

Adapted and published by GRANGIS under the OGL Licence 3.0.

www.nationalarchives.gov.uk/doc/open-government-licence/version/3/

GRANGIS - UK PUBLISHING 2022.

Thank you for taking the time to leave us a review regarding this version

★★★★★

For further inquiries, contact us at:
www.grangis.com / contact@grangis.com

www.ingramcontent.com/pod-product-compliance
Lightning Source LLC
LaVergne TN
LVHW060214210926
848481LV00008B/2734